THE FILM CLASSICS LIBRARY

CASABLANCA

Edited by Richard J. Anobile

A DARIEN HOUSE BOOK

FLARE BOOKS/PUBLISHED BY AVON

A DARIEN HOUSE BOOK

AVON BOOKS
A division of
The Hearst Corporation
959 Eighth Avenue
New York, New York 10019

Published by arrangement with
Darien House, Inc.
37 Riverside Drive
New York City 10023

Library of Congress Catalog Card Number: 74-82132

ISBN 0-380-00086-5

First Flare Printing, September 1974.

FLARE TRADEMARK REG. U.S. PAT. OFF. AND
OTHER COUNTRIES. MARCA REGISTRADA,
HECHO EN U.S.A.

Printed in the United States of America

Introduction

The piano strikes up "As Time Goes By" and soon afterward Humphrey Bogart storms into Rick's for his fateful reunion with Ingrid Bergman. The facade the screenwriters have painstakingly built around Bogart's character throughout the first two reels rapidly crumbles. It is soon apparent that Rick, the rugged American individualist, has a sentimental streak which will plague him to the last fade-out. Now we may be at the heart of CASABLANCA. The universal struggle of all men to fight off emotional feelings; to be men in a traditional role. To his credit, Rick allows those feelings to run rampant. Without a doubt, Bogart turns in his most sensitive performance as he portrays a man torn by his own needs and those of society.

And that's another plausible interpretation of one aspect of CASABLANCA. Books are stuffed with the 'real meaning' of the film. The screenwriters, I am sure, are caught by surprise every time they see someone's interpretation. After all, they didn't know, until the last scene was shot, how the film would resolve itself. Yet, despite the confusion on the CASABLANCA set, the film which evolved is an undisputed classic with wide appeal.

Here is the complete CASABLANCA. Not just a script with a few meaningless stills bound into the center, but the entire film reconstructed through the use of over 1400 frame blowups. The basic shortcoming of those plentiful script books which clutter bookstore shelves is that it is very unnatural to read dialogue and camera directions of a film already produced. The characterizations brought to the film by the actors are lost along with the subtle remarks of the director's camera. Here, almost every aspect of the film is presented to give you a complete record of CASABLANCA in book form. I am pleased to be able to add CASABLANCA to the Film Classics Library and am grateful to have also been able to have had a conversation with Ms. Ingrid Bergman. I hope the interview which follows will give you an interesting insight into the making of this film.

Richard J. Anobile
New York City
June, 1974

...With Ingrid Bergman

RICHARD J. ANOBILE: *When did you first hear about* CASABLANCA?

INGRID BERGMAN: In Hollywood, about 33 years ago. I was under contract to David Selznick but he didn't do many pictures directly with me. He made a few pictures, always very good ones, but he rented me out to other studios. I had done INTERMEZZO for him. Then I did ADAM AND HIS FOUR SONS, RAGE IN HEAVEN and DR. JEKYLL AND MR. HYDE. I always played parts such as a refugee or a little girl.

One day he called me up and said, "I have a marvelous part for you. Warner Bros. is doing a picture called CASABLANCA and you are going to be the most marvelous woman in Casablanca." So I went over to his office and said, "So, what is the story?" "Oh," he said, "I don't quite know what the story is, but I'm so glad you are going to be beautifully dressed and you are going to have a beautiful entrance." Well, I was a little mad and said, "You cannot sell me for something when you don't know the story! Maybe the part isn't any good."

There were two brothers who wrote the script, the Epstein brothers. Selznick said that he had confidence in them and that they were coming over to tell us the story. And they came and they were very vague about the story. They had an idea but it was all "maybe we'll do it this way" and "we'll probably do that" and "we're going to get a good cast." And indeed, they got a very good cast. Every little part was played by an excellent actor. And then we began shooting.

5

I didn't know from one day to the other what we were going to do. I was quite upset sometimes. It was a film that had only a skeleton and we worked on it day by day. Michael Curtiz, the director, would have big fights with the producer because even he didn't know where the story was going.

I had a problem as there were two men, played by Paul Henreid and Humphrey Bogart, who were both in love with me. So I said to the writers, "Now which of these two men do I end up with?" And they said, "We haven't decided yet so we are going to shoot it two ways." "But this is impossible," I said. "You must tell me because, after all, there is a little bit of difference in acting towards a man that you love and another man for whom you may just feel pity or affection." "Well," they said, "don't give too much of anything. Play it in between, just, you know, so that we can decide in the end." Well, there was nothing for me to do but go ahead and try to play it in between. We came to the end of the picture—actually we were going to shoot two ends: one where I would go with Paul Henreid in the plane and one where I would stay on the ground with Humphrey Bogart and Henreid would fly away.

Well, we shot the first ending, the one where Claude Rains and Humphrey Bogart walk away in the fog. When we finished the scene we were told that that was it and there was no need to shoot the other ending. With all that confusion we had very little belief in the movie. To our great surprise it won the Academy Award.

I hadn't seen the picture in its entire length for maybe 30 years when in London—at the British Film Institute —they asked me to come down and lecture on it. So I said, "Well, I don't know if I can lecture on it but I'll come down and maybe if the audience wants to know something I can answer questions." And when I saw it and came up on stage the first thing I said was, "What a good movie that was!" That seemed very strange to the audience, but they laughed.

ANOBILE: *Did you have any preference as to which ending should be shot?*

BERGMAN: No, I think that this was the best. I mean, I think the other ending would have been very disappointing.

What about the other members of the cast, or prominent members, say Bogart, did he mind the fact that obviously every day he was handed a different script or changes in the current script?

Yes, there would be changes in the scenes, maybe a couple of pages, it was all back and forth. No, I don't think he was very pleased about it. Very many people ask me how well I knew him, and you know, was I fond of him or something. And I always say, "No, I kissed him but I don't know him!" He was very much by himself and I think he was very worried about it. He used to go into his little

trailer on the set and close the door and he had his friends and the people around him and business men and so on. But he wasn't sitting around on the set and making jokes and was not in a very happy mood. But he was an excellent companion because he always worked very hard and was very concerned about our scenes. When you see the picture now you realize what an enormous talent he had with that rough, tough way, yet he brings out so much love.

I assume that there was no such thing as location shooting—that the whole thing was shot on the Warner Bros. lot.

Yes, and I was so upset about always doing everything on a back lot. Everything was false. All the Arabs and all the people of Casablanca were dressed-up extras. I remember pleading with the producer and the director, asking if we could go to Casablanca and shoot the real scene. But, of course, the war was on so it wasn't easy to travel to Casablanca. But it was all done on the back lot and they built a whole set there.

When Selznick first came to you and told you that he had this fantastic script or story for you, did you have any ideas at all that you would be working opposite Bogart?

Yes, I knew that because that was one of the reasons that Mr. Selznick was anxious for me to accept the movie. It was all written for Bogart, and Claude Rains, I think, was also already cast. When the others were approached for their different parts I don't know, but I knew that Bogart was going to be my leading man.

Did that make you anxious to accept the role?

Yes, I wanted very much to work with him but I was frightened of him because I had seen all those movies. He always played the villain and he looked like a very tough man and if you were not a friend of his you had a feeling he was going to knock you over. But I saw THE MALTESE FALCON over and over again so I could get used to him so that when I met him I wouldn't be so frightened.

Did he have any specific way of working which might have been strange or unusual? Was he the kind of actor who would come on the set and do his work or did he have to get into the role?

No, not at all. No, the method acting had, I think, just started. This was an idea that came up much later. No, he was just a natural actor and had no complications with getting into the mood. He was always in the mood.

The one thing that I have heard was that there was a lot of criticism of the pairing of Ingrid Bergman and Humphrey Bogart. People felt that the chemistry just wouldn't work. Did you hear anything about that at the time or is it just another Hollywood myth?

I have never heard that. I have heard just the opposite, that it was a very good combination.

No, no, not after the movie, but prior, people seemed to have doubts as to whether or not it would be a very good combination.

Well now, I didn't know anything about that. Even if they talked about it I didn't hear it, luckily enough.

Were there any reasons why you never worked again with Bogart?

No.

Yet, I would think that it would have been logical, after the success of CASABLANCA. *Hollywood always tried to bring the same people together again.*

Well, no, it never came up. I worked very much and had very good leading men in my whole ten years of Hollywood, but for some strange reason it didn't happen. I mean he did many movies and I don't know, I think sometimes you wish to work together again, then you try to get together again. So, for instance, with Cary Grant I managed to do more than one and with Gary Cooper we did two and with Charles Boyer we did two. But with Humphrey Bogart it never worked out.

When did you last see Bogart?

I saw him the last time in Italy. I think he was working on a picture called BEAT THE DEVIL with John Huston. We had supper together with other friends and he was a little bit upset about my having left Hollywood. He felt sorry for me because he thought I had ruined my career by stepping away from the Hollywood scene and into Italian movies. In those days the Italian movies that I made were not successful. Now when they are shown on television they are supposed to be masterpieces. So, if you wait long enough people change their opinion. So I said to him, "Well, I am a very happy woman and maybe that is just as important as being a box office success in America."

How did you get on with the director, Michael Curtiz? Did you have any problems because of the script or . . .

No, he was—as I say, everybody was a little bit irritated by this kind of writing day by day. But he was an excellent director and very sweet and nice to me. He stayed a friend until he passed away.

Do you remember any interesting things that ended up on the cutting room floor and were not in the final version?

No, I can't remember that. I don't remember any of those details of it. I remember one thing, though, that I thought was very clever. That is, the airport. They wanted a tremendous long view of this airport and the little plane coming in, so they had midgets in the background so that the people would look very small. I thought that was a very clever idea.

From the script I have, I get the impression that the airport was a miniature.

Yes, that's possible. Of course, I was never in on those technical parts.

You know, in Paris, when the picture came out they weren't pleased with it. They didn't like the political point of view. The picture was taken off immediately and was never sold to television. A while ago it was brought in and opened in *five* theaters in Paris, as a new movie. They had a big gala opening where I appeared and people were absolutely crazy about it. So it is very strange; it isn't anything nostalgic when you remember you saw it thirty years ago and you'd like to see it again. It just took the French with great enthusiasm, which shows that it is still a picture that has not aged. And luckily my hair . . . Very often hair and hats age you tremendously and look quite ridiculous a couple of years later. But the two hats I wear are classical hats that you can wear today, and the clothes—it was the period when you had those very big shoulders, but as I was very big shouldered I didn't have to fill them out anymore—so the clothes looked quite nice. They are really clothes you can wear today, which is very nice, otherwise you sit there with a little smile because women's clothes age so quickly.

Did you have any say in the selection of the clothes?

Of course, yes, there are always designs made and then you discuss them with the director and the producer and you all agree on which one to use. Every dress I wear in CASABLANCA I could wear today.

Have you seen Woody Allen's PLAY IT AGAIN, SAM?

Yes, of course I have. And I wanted to check if—to see who said "play it again Sam." And when I saw the movie, I listened for it and realized that none of us said "play it again Sam." But I did see the movie and thought it was very funny.

I think the closest to it is when you tell Sam to play it.

Yes, but I only say "play it Sam." I don't say "again."

So nobody says "play it again Sam." Well, I guess that's a better film title than PLAY IT SAM. *When you look at* CASABLANCA—*and I don't know if you are still a movie fan today, I assume you are?*

Yes.

Why do you think CASABLANCA *still has appeal today?*

I think because of the sentimental things, and the glorification with the "Marseillaise" being sung and all that. I think that's what people like. I think they miss that in modern films. You have everything in that movie from love to heroism and murder and whatnot. I think it has a beautiful tempo. I notice how modern movies drag out. They keep the camera on a scene and they enjoy the scenery and people are silent and think and . . . But there is so much action in CASABLANCA. The picture is cut in such a way that there is never a dull moment. There isn't a foot of film that is too long.

Were there any instances where you or Bogart might just improvise a scene?

No, I don't think we did that. It was always discussed with the writers. Michael Curtiz spent most of his lunch hour with the producer discussing the dialogue. I can't remember that anything was improvised. We learned the lines when we got them.

Did you ever see the stage version of CASABLANCA?

A play? I didn't know that. Are you sure?

Yes, it's from an original play titled Everybody Goes to Rick's. *I'm not sure if it was produced on Broadway but I was wondering if you had ever seen the original because it struck me as curious that the writers would say they didn't really have a script when they at least had an original story.*

Well, I didn't know that and I have never read anything except the script of CASABLANCA and I actually thought it was their original idea. But then if the play was produced or not produced, I wouldn't know. Maybe they got the idea and changed it around because I never knew it was based on anything.

The title of the play is incorporated in a line spoken in the film by Claude Rains. The original playwrights are credited in the film.

Is that in the credits?

Yes.

Isn't that funny, I didn't notice that when I saw the movie recently.

How was the film initially received?

Oh, very well. Otherwise I am sure it would not have been up for an award. When it was up for an award—I don't know what the other pictures were like, that would be nice to find out.

I understand that CASABLANCA *slowly picked up momentum, then snowballed.*

Yes, I think that's true. It snowballed. However, it must have been good to come up for nomination, I mean maybe it didn't hit people as much as it has lately. Friends here in New York, where you very often have CASABLANCA on television, tell me that they have seen it eight times and each time they plan to watch only a little bit of it and they get stuck and they look at the whole thing again. People just can't turn it off! And you wouldn't be doing this book if the picture were not something quite sensational.

Acknowledgments

I would like to take this opportunity to thank those individuals and organizations whose cooperation have made this book possible. Rights to produce this book were granted to us by Warner Bros. Pictures and United Artists Television. Sidney Kiwitt, Leo Wilder and Stanley Belkin of Warner Bros. and Jack Benjamin and Bart Farber of United Artists were especially helpful in sorting out legal tangles. I would also like to acknowledge Ms. Eve Baer and Mr. Jack McLaughlin of United Artists for their assistance in making materials available to me.

Alyne Model and George Norris of Riverside Film Associates transferred my marks to negative material and attended to the nitty-gritty of that highly technical job. All blowups were produced at Vita Print in New York City.

Harry Chester Associates was responsible for the design. I would also like to thank Warner Bros. Music for giving us permission to use lyrics for "As Time Goes By," especially Mr. Al Kohn of that organization. Ms. Angela Freytag patiently worked with me in getting all the German down pat where it was omitted from the script and Mr. Bernard Jacobson worked out the French. Their valued help allowed me to remain as true as possible to the original film and for that I am grateful. Finally, I'd like to say thank you to Ms. Vivien Rowan of Darien House for her all-around help, especially in fitting together the many loose ends about which I'm so damn sloppy.

RICHARD J. ANOBILE

Note to reader:

In keeping as true to the film as possible I have left in lap dissolves and fades where I felt they were necessary. The effect of a lap dissolve to the reader will be the appearance of two seemingly superimposed photos. The purpose here—as it was the director's, is to bridge the time and place gap between two scenes.

You will also notice a fuzziness in some frames. This is due to the fact that every photo is taken from blow-ups of the film itself. All possible means have been taken to insure clarity but inconsistencies in negative quality account for the variations of photo densities you will observe.

Screen Play by
JULIUS J. and PHILIP G. EPSTEIN
HOWARD KOCH

From a Play by
MURRAY BURNETT
and JOAN ALISON

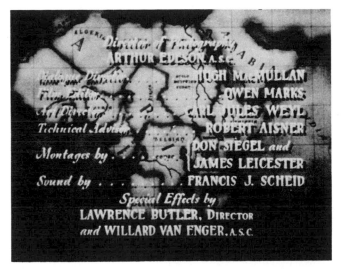

Director of Photography
ARTHUR EDESON, A.S.C.
HUGH MacMULLAN
OWEN MARKS
CARL JULES WEYL
Technical Adviser
ROBERT AISNER
DON SIEGEL and
Montages by
JAMES LEICESTER
Sound by
FRANCIS J. SCHEID
Special Effects by
LAWRENCE BUTLER, Director
and WILLARD VAN ENGER, A.S.C.

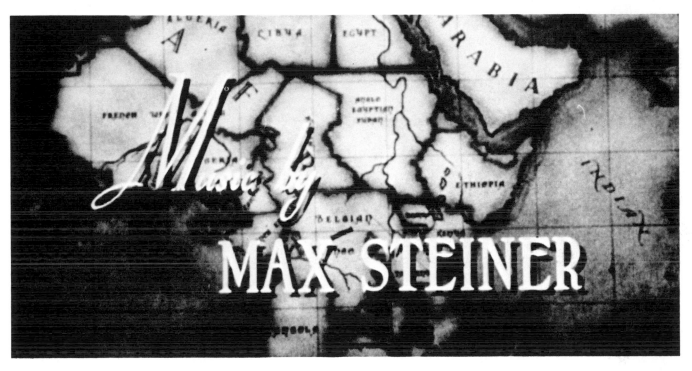

Music by
MAX STEINER

A
HAL B. WALLIS
PRODUCTION

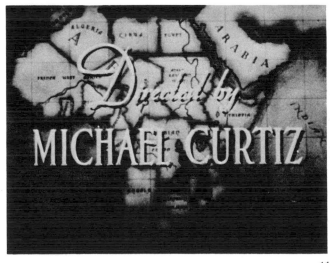

Directed by
MICHAEL CURTIZ

Narrator: With the coming of the second World War,

Narrator: many eyes in imprisoned Europe turned hopefully or desperately toward the freedom of the Americas.

Narrator: Lisbon became the great embarkation point. But not everybody could get to Lisbon directly.

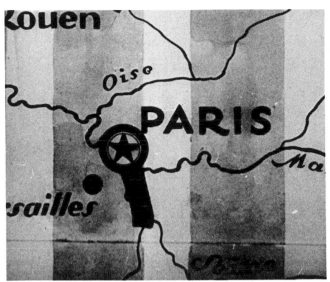

Narrator: And so a tortuous, roundabout refugee trail sprang up.

Paris to Marseilles . . .

Narrator: Across the Mediterranean

Narrator: to Oran . . .

Narrator: Then by train or auto or foot across the rim of Africa to Casablanca in French Morocco.

Narrator: Here the fortunate ones through money or influence or luck, might obtain exit visas and scurry to Lisbon.

13

Narrator: And from Lisbon to the new world.

Narrator: But the others wait in Casablanca and wait and wait and wait.

Operator: . . . To all officials. Two German couriers carrying important official documents murdered on train Murderer and possible accomplices headed for Casablanca. Round up all suspicious characters and search them for stolen documents!! Important!

Officer: En avant garcons!

15

2nd Officer: Allez! Au wagon! Allez!
Toute suite. Rentrez! Apres! Apres!

Policeman: May we see your papers?

Traveler: I don't think I have them on me.
Policeman: In that case we'll have to ask
you to come along.

Traveler: Well, it's possible that I—

Traveler: Yes. Here they are.

Policeman: These papers expired
three weeks ago.

Policeman: You'll have to come along—

Policeman: Halt!

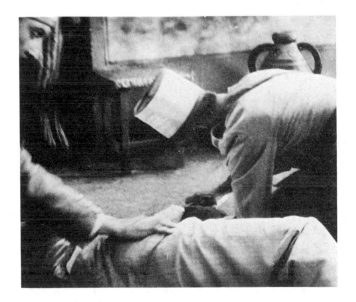

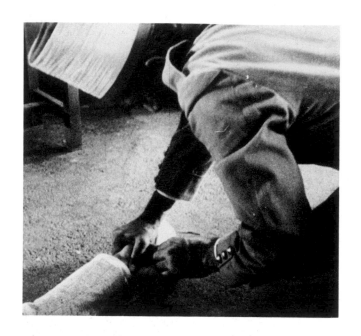

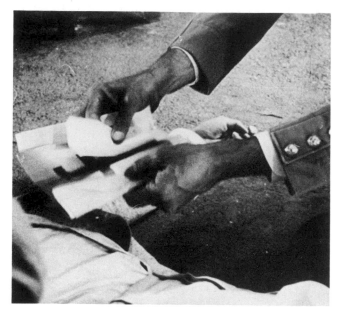

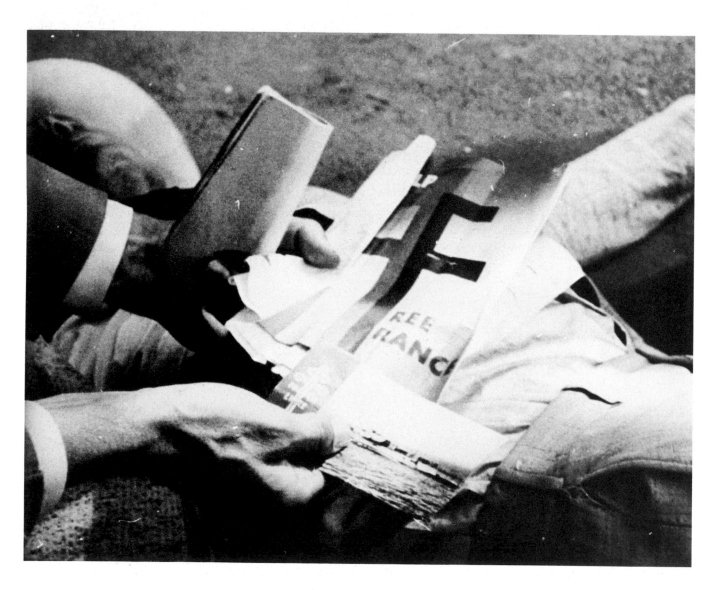

Woman: What on earth's going on there?
Husband: I don't know, my dear.

Foreigner: Pardon me, pardon me, monsieur. Pardon, madame. Have you not heard?
Husband: We hear very little and understand even less.

Foreigner: Two German couriers were found murdered in the desert, the unoccupied desert.

Foreigner: This is the customary roundup of refugees, liberals and, of course, a beautiful young girl for Monsieur Renault, the Prefect of Police . . .

Foreigner: Unfortunately, along with these unhappy refugees, the scum of Europe has **gravitated** to Casablanca. Some of them have been waiting years for a visa.

Foreigner: I beg of you, monsieur. Watch **yourself**. Be on guard. This place is full of vultures. Vultures! Everywhere! Everywhere!

Husband: Oh, er, thank you. Thank you very much.
Foreigner: Not at all. Au revoir, Monsieur. Au revoir, Madame.

Husband: Au revoir! Amusing little fella! Huh?
Woman: Yes?
Husband: Waiter?

Husband: Oh! How silly of me!
Woman: What, dear?

Husband: I've left my wallet in the hotel!
Woman: Oh—
Husband: I—

Annina: Perhaps tomorrow we'll be on the plane.

Officer: Attention!

Heinze: Heil, Hitler!
Officers: Heil, Hitler!

Heinze: It is very good to see you again, Major Strasser.
Strasser: Thank you. Thank you.

Heinze: May I present Captain Renault, Police Prefect of Casablanca. Major Strasser.

Renault: Unoccupied France welcomes you to Casablanca.

Strasser: Thank you, captain. It's very good to be here.

Renault: Major Strasser, my aide, Lieutenant Casselle.

Tonelli: Captain Tonelli. The Italian service is at your command, Major.

Renault: You may find the climate of Casablanca a trifle warm, Major.

Strasser: Oh, we Germans must get used to all climates from Russia to the Sahara. But, perhaps, you were not referring to the weather?

Renault: What else, my dear Major?
Strasser: By the way, the murder of the couriers, what has been done?
Renault: Oh, realizing the importance of the case, my men are rounding up twice the usual number of suspects.

Heinze: We know already who the murderer is.
Strasser: Good. Is he in custody?

Renault: Oh, there's no hurry. Tonight he'll be at Rick's. Everybody comes to Rick's.
Strasser: I have already heard about this cafe. And also about Mr. Rick himself!

25

Man: . . . Waiting, waiting, waiting. I'll never get out of here. I'll die in Casablanca.

Girl: But can't you make it just a little more, please?
Moor: I'm sorry, madame. But diamonds are a drug on the market. Everybody sells diamonds. There are diamonds everywhere. Two thousand, four hundred—
Girl: All right.

Man: The trucks are waiting, the men are waiting—
German tourist: I don't understand the whole thing; one should have a much stronger hand here in Casablanca.

Older man: It's the fishing smack, Santiago. It leaves at one tomorrow night, here from the end of La Medina. The third boat.
Refugee: Thank you, thank you.
Older man: And bring the fifteen thousand francs in cash. Remember, in cash.

Sacha: Cheerio! Bottoms up!
Man: Cheerio!

Carl: Open up, Abdul.
Abdul: Yes, Herr Professor.

Italian woman: Grazie, signor.

28

Chinese: Don't worry. I've arranged everything.

Woman guest: Er, waiter?
Carl: Yes, madame?
Guest: Will you ask **Rick** if he'll have a drink with us?

Carl: Madame, he never drinks with customers. Never! I have never seen him.

Guest: Oh.
Woman: What makes saloonkeepers so snobbish?

Man: Perhaps if you told him I ran the second largest banking house in Amsterdam.
Carl: Second largest? That wouldn't impress Rick.

Carl: The leading banker in Amsterdam is now the pastry chef in our kitchen.
Woman: Oh!

Man: We have something to look forward to.

Carl: And his father is the bellboy.

Abdul: I'm sorry, sir. This is a private room.

German: Of all the nerve! Who do you think—I know there is gambling in there. There is no secret! You dare not keep me out of here.

Rick: Yes? What's the trouble?
Abdul: Er, this gentleman—
German: I have been in every gambling room between Honolulu and Berlin.

German: If you think I'm going to be kept out of a saloon like this, you're very much mistaken.

Ugarte: Er, excuse me, please.

Ugarte: Hello, Rick.

Rick: Your cash is good at the bar.
German: What? Do you know who I am?

Rick: I do. You're lucky the bar's open to you.

German: This **is** outrageous! I shall report it to the Angriff.

Ugarte: Huh. You know, Rick, watching you just now with the Deutschebank, one would think you'd been doing this all your life.

Rick: Well, what makes you think I haven't?
Ugarte: Oh, nothing. Huh. Er, but when you first came to Casablanca, I thought—

Rick: You thought what?
Ugarte: What right do I have to think?

Ugarte: May I?

Ugarte: Too bad about those two German couriers, wasn't it?

Rick: They got a lucky break. Yesterday they were just two German clerks. Today they're the honored dead.

Ugarte: You are a very cynical person, Rick, if you'll forgive me for saying so.
Rick: I forgive you.

Ugarte: Er, thank you. Will you have a drink with me, please?
Rick: No!
Ugarte: Oh, I forgot, you never drink with . . .But then I, I'll have another, please.
Waiter: Yes, Monsieur.

Ugarte: You despise me, don't you?
Rick: Well, if I gave you any thought, I probably would.

Ugarte: But why? Oh, you object to the kind of business I do, huh?

Ugarte: But, but think of all those poor refugees who must rot in this place if I didn't help them. Well, that's not so bad.

Ugarte: Through ways of my own I provide them with exit visas.

Rick: For a price, Ugarte, for a price.

Ugarte: But think of all the poor devils who can't meet Renault's price.

Ugarte: So I get it for them for half. Is that so parasitic?

Rick: I don't mind a parasite.

Rick: I object to a cut-rate one.

Ugarte: Well, Rick, after tonight I'll be through with the whole business and I'm leaving finally, this Casablanca.

39

Rick: Who'd you bribe for your visa? Renault or yourself?

Ugarte: Myself. I found myself much more reasonable.

Ugarte: Look, Rick. Do you know what this is?

Ugarte: Something that even you have never seen. Letters of Transit signed by General de Gaulle.

Ugarte: They cannot be rescinded, not even questioned.

Ugarte: Tonight I'll be selling these for more money than even I have ever dreamed of.

Ugarte: And then, addio Casablanca!

Ugarte: You know, Rick, I have many friends in Casablanca, but somehow just because you despise me, you are the only one I trust.

Ugarte: Will you keep these for me, please?
Rick: For how long?

Ugarte: Oh, perhaps for an hour, perhaps a little longer.
Rick: I don't want them here overnight.

Ugarte: Oh, don't be afraid of that. Keep them for me. Thank you. I knew I could trust you.

Ugarte: Oh, waiter! I'll be expecting some people. If, er, anybody asks for me, I'll be right here.
Waiter: Yes, Monsieur.

Ugarte: Rick, I hope you're more impressed with me now. If you'll forgive me I'll share my good luck with your roulette wheel.

Rick: Just a moment.

Rick: I heard a rumor those two German couriers were carrying letters of transit.

Ugarte: Huh? Oh, huh, I heard that rumor, too. Poor devils.

Rick: Yes. You're right, Ugarte. I am a little more impressed with you.

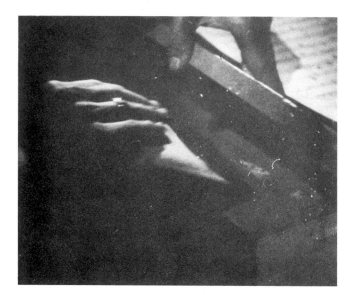

Ferrari: Hello, Rick.
Rick: Hello, Ferrari. How's business at the Blue Parrot?
Ferrari: Fine, but I'd like to buy your cafe.
Rick: It's not for sale.

Ferrari: You haven't heard my offer.
Rick: It's not for sale at any price.
Ferrari: What do you want for Sam?
Rick: I don't buy or sell human beings.

Ferrari: That's too bad. That's Casablanca's leading commodity. In refugees alone we could make a fortune if you'd work with me through the black market.

Rick: Suppose you run your business and let me run mine?

Ferrari: Suppose we ask Sam. Maybe he'd like to make a change.
Rick: Suppose we do.

Ferrari: My dear Rick, when will you realize that in this world, today, isolationism is no longer a practical policy?

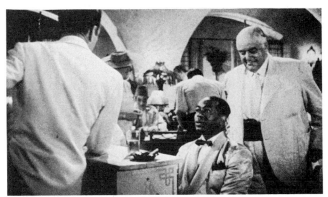

Rick: Sam, Ferrari wants you to work for him at the Blue Parrot.
Sam: Oh, Ah like it fine heah.

Rick: He'll double what I pay you.
Sam: Yeah, but Ah ain't got time to spend the money Ah make heah.

Rick: Sorry.

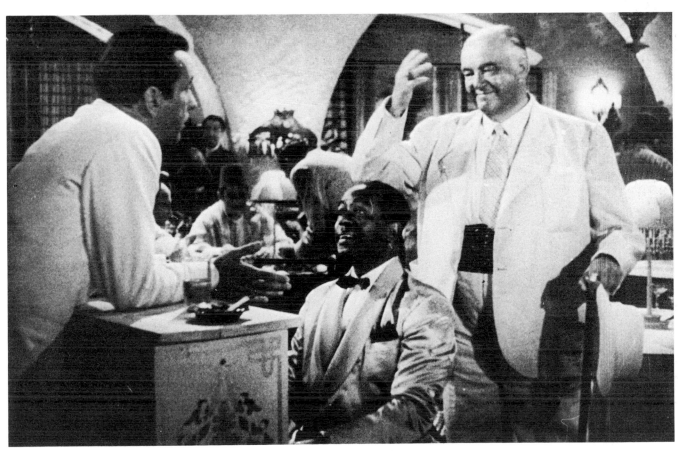

Sacha: The boss's private stock. Because Yvonne, I love you.
Yvonne: Oh, shut up!

Sacha: All right, all right!

Sacha: For you I shut up, because Yvonne, I love you. Clk! Clk! Oh-oh!

Sacha: Oh, Monsieur Rick. Monsieur Rick. Some Germans, boom, boom, boom, boom, give this check.

Sacha: Is it all right?

Yvonne: Where were you last night?
Rick: That's so long ago I don't remember.
Yvonne: Will I see you tonight?
Rick: I never make plans that far ahead.

Yvonne: Give me another.
Rick: Sacha, she's had enough.
Yvonne: Don't listen to him, Sacha. Fill it up.

Sacha: Yvonne, I love you, but he pays me.

Yvonne: Rick, I'm sick and tired of having you—
Rick: Sacha, call a cab.
Sacha: Yes, boss.

Rick: Come on, we're going to get your coat.
Yvonne: Take your hands off me!
Rick: No you're going home. You've had a little too much to drink.

Sacha: Hey, taxi!

Yvonne: Who do you think you are, pushing me around? What a fool I was to fall for a man like you.

Rick: Go with her, Sacha, and be sure she gets home.
Sacha: Yes, boss.
Rick: And come right back.
Sacha: Yes, boss.

Renault: Hello, Rick!
Rick: Hello, Louis.

Renault: How extravagant you are, throwing away women like that. Someday they may be scarce.
Renault: You know, *I* think now I shall pay a call on Yvonne. Maybe get her on the rebound, huh?
Rick: Well, when it comes to women, you're a true democrat.

Officier: Vous n'auriez rien pu accomplir sans les armées allemandes. Ft la Grèce, ce pauvre petit pays de Grèce, mon cher, mais . . .

Renault: If he gets a word in it'll be a major Italian victory.

Renault: The plane to Lisbon.

Renault: You'd like to be on it?
Rick: Why? What's in Lisbon?

Renault: The Clipper to America. **I've** often speculated on why you **don't** return to America.

Renault: Did you abscond with the church funds? Did you run off with the Senator's wife?

Renault: I'd like to think that you killed a man. It's the romantic in me.

Rick: It was a combination of all three.
Renault: And what in heaven's name brought you to Casablanca?
Rick: My health. I came to Casablanca for the waters.

Renault: What waters? We're in the desert.
Rick: I was misinformed.
Renault: Huh?

Croupier: Excuse me, Monsieur Rick. But a gentleman inside has won twenty thousand francs, and the cashier would like some money.
Rick: Well, I'll get it from the safe.

Croupier: I'm so upset, Monsieur Rick. You know I . . .
Rick: All right, Emile. Mistakes like that happen all the time.
Croupier: I'm awfully sorry.

Renault: Rick! There's gonna be some excitement here tonight. We're gonna make an arrest in your cafe.
Rick: What, again?

Renault: Oh, this is no ordinary arrest. A murderer, no less. If you're thinking of warning him, don't put yourself out. He cannot possibly escape.

Rick: I stick my neck out for nobody.

Renault: A wise foreign policy.

Renault: We could have made this arrest earlier in the evening at the Blue Parrot. But out of my high regard for you, we're staging it here. It will amuse your customers.
Rick: Our entertainment's enough.

Renault: Rick, we're to have an important guest here tonight. Major Strasser of the Third Reich, no less. We want to arrest the man when he is here. A little demonstration of the efficiency of my administration.

Rick: I see. And what's Strasser doing here? He certainly didn't come all the way to Casablanca to witness a demonstration of your efficiency.
Renault: Perhaps not.

Rick: Here you are.
Emile: It shall not happen again, monsieur.
Rick: That's all right.

Rick: Yeah? Have a brandy?

Rick: Louis, you've got something on your mind. Why don't you spill it?
Renault: How observant you are. As a matter of fact, I wanted to give you a word of advice.

Renault: Thank you. Rick. there are many exit visas sold in this café, but we know that you've never sold one. That is the reason we permit you to remain open.

Rick: Oh, I thought it was because I let you win at roulette.
Renault: Er, that is another reason. There is a man arrived in Casablanca on his way to America. He will offer a fortune to anyone who'll furnish him with an exit visa.

Rick: Yeah? What's his name?
Renault: Victor Laszlo!

Rick: Victor Laszlo?

Renault: Rick, that is the first time I've ever seen you so impressed.
Rick: Well, he's succeeded in impressing half the world.

Renault: It's my duty to see that he doesn't impress the other half. Rick, Laszlo must never reach America. He stays in Casablanca.
Rick: It'll be interesting to see how he manages.

Renault: Manages what?
Rick: His escape.
Renault: Oh, but I just told you—

Rick: Stop it. He escaped from a concentration camp and the Nazis have been chasing him all over Europe.
Renault: This is the end of the chase.

Rick: Twenty thousand francs says it isn't.

Renault: Is that a serious offer?

Rick: I just paid out twenty. I'd like to get it back.

Renault: Make it ten. I'm only a poor corrupt official.
Rick: Okay.

Renault: Done. No matter how clever he is, he still needs an exit visa. Or I should say, two.

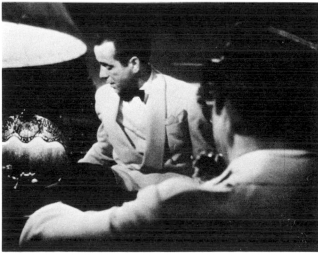

Rick: Why two?
Renault: He is traveling with a lady.
Rick: Well, he'll take one.

Renault: I think not. I've seen the lady. And if he did not leave her in Marseilles or Oran, he certainly won't leave her in Casablanca.

Rick: Well, maybe he's not quite as romantic as you are.

Renault: It doesn't matter. There is no exit visa for him.

Rick: Louis, whatever gave you the impression that I might be interested in helping Laszlo escape?

Renault: Because, my dear Ricky, I suspect that under that cynical shell you're at heart a sentimentalist. Oh, laugh if you will, but I happen to be familiar with your record. Let me point out just two items.

Renault: In 1935, you ran guns to Ethiopia.

Renault: In 1936, you fought in Spain on the Loyalist side.

Rick: And got paid well for it on both occasions.

Renault: The winning side would have paid you much better.
Rick: Maybe . . . .

Rick: Well, it seems that you're determined to keep Laszlo here.

Renault: I have my orders.
Rick: Oh, I see. Gestapo spank.

Renault: My dear Ricky, you overestimate the influence of the Gestapo. I don't interfere with them and they don't interfere with me. In Casablanca, I'm master of my fate. I am captain—

Aide: Major Strasser is here, sir.
Rick: Yeah, as you were saying.

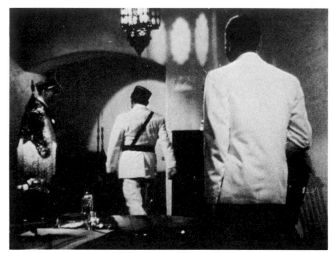

Renault: Excuse me.

Renault: Carl. See that Major Strasser gets a good table, one close to the ladies.

Carl: I have already given him the best; knowing he is German and would take it anyway.

Renault: Take him quietly. Two guards at every door.

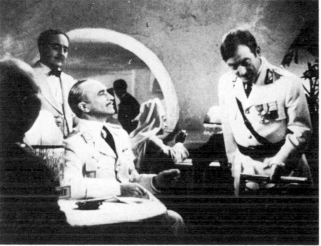 

Renault: Good evening, gentlemen.
Strasser: Good evening, captain.
Heinze: Won't you join us?
Renault: Thank you. It's a pleasure to have you here, major.

Strasser: Er, champagne and a tin of caviar.

Renault: Er, may I recommend Veuve Cliquot '26, a good French wine?
Strasser: Thank you.
Waiter: Very well, sir.

Strasser: A very interesting club.
Renault: Er, especially so tonight, major. In a few minutes, you will see the arrest of the man who murdered your couriers.
Strasser: I expected no less, Captain.

Officer: Monsieur Ugarte?

Ugarte: Oh!

Officer: Will you please come with us?

Ugarte: Certainly.

Ugarte: May I first please cash my chips?

Ugarte: Very lucky, huh? Two thousand, please.
Banker: Two thousand.

Ugarte: Thank you.

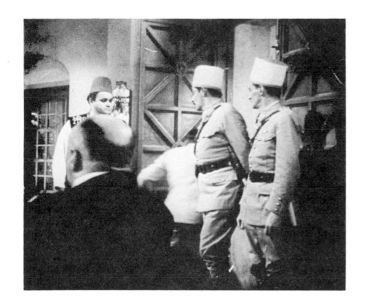

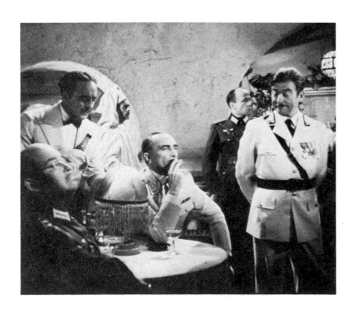

Ugarte: Rick! Rick! Rick!

Rick: Don't be a fool. You can't get away!
Ugarte: But, Rick, hide me! Do something! You must help me, Rick! Do something!
Rick: Shut up!

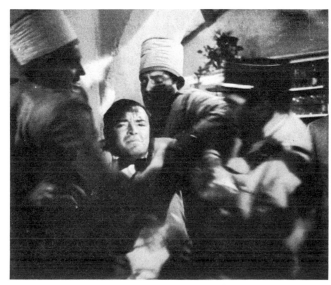

Ugarte: RICK! RICK!

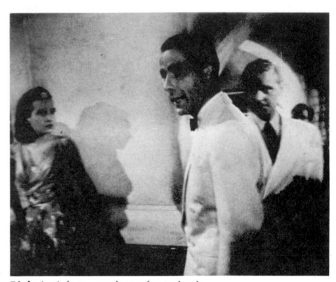

Strasser: Excellent, Captain.

Gambler: When they come to get me, Rick, I hope you'll be more of a help!

Rick: I stick my neck out for nobody.

Rick: I'm sorry there was a disturbance, folks. But it's all over now. Everything's all right. Just sit down and have a good time. Enjoy yourselves.

Rick: All right, Sam.
Sam: Okay, boss.

Renault: Oh, Rick? Rick?

Renault: Er, this is Major Heinrich Strasser of the Third Reich.

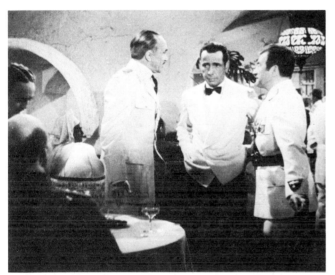

Strasser: How do you do, Mr. Rick?
Rick: Oh, how do you do.

Renault: And you already know Herr Heinze of the Third Reich?
Strasser: Please join us, Mr. Rick.

Renault: We are very honored tonight, Rick. Major Strasser is one of the reasons the Third Reich enjoys the reputation it has today.

Strasser: You repeat *Third* Reich as though you expected there to be others.
Renault: Well, personally, Major, I will take what comes.

Strasser: Do you mind if I ask you a few questions? Unofficially, of course.
Rick: Make it official if you like.
Strasser: What is your nationality?

Rick: I'm a drunkard.

Renault: And that makes Rick a citizen of the world.

Rick: I was born in New York City if that'll help you any.
Strasser: I understand that you came here from Paris at the time of the occupation.

Rick: Well, there seems to be no secret about that.

Strasser: Are you one of those people who cannot imagine the Germans in their beloved Paris?

Rick: It's not particularly *my* beloved Paris.

Heinze: Can you imagine us in London?

Rick: When you get there, ask me.

Renault: Oh! Diplomatist!
Strasser: How about New York?

Rick: Well, there are certain sections of New York, Major, that I wouldn't advise you try to invade.
Strasser: Hm-huh. Who do you think will win the war?
Rick: I haven't the slightest idea.

Renault: Rick is completely neutral about everything. And that takes in the field of women, too.

74

Strasser: You were not always so carefully neutral. We have a complete dossier on you.

Strasser: "Richard Blaine, American, Age 37. Cannot return to his country." The reason is a little vague.

Strasser: We also know what you did in Paris, Mr. Blaine, and also we know why you left Paris. Don't worry. We are not going to broadcast it.

Rick: Hmmm. Are my eyes really brown?

Strasser: You will forgive my curiosity, Mr. Blaine. The point is, an enemy of the Reich has come to Casablanca and we are checking up on anyone who can be of any help to us.

Rick: Well, my interest in whether Victor Laszlo stays or goes is purely a sporting one.

Strasser: In this case, you have no sympathy for the fox, huh?

Rick: Not particularly. I understand the point of view of the hound, too.

Strasser: Victor Laszlo published the foulest lies in the Prague newspapers until the very day **we marched in**. And even after that, he continued to print scandal sheets in a cellar.

Renault: Of course, one must admit he has great courage.

Strasser: I admit he's very clever. Three times he slipped through our fingers. **In Paris** he continued his activities. We intend not to let it happen again.

Rick: Er, you'll excuse me, **gentlemen**? Your business is politics. Mine is **running a saloon**.
Strasser: Good evening, Mr. Blaine.

76

Renault: You see, Major, you have nothing to worry about Rick.
Strasser: Perhaps.

Waiter: Yes, monsieur.
Laszlo: I reserved a table. Victor Laszlo.
Waiter: Yes, Monsieur Laszlo. Right this way.

Laszlo: Two Cointreaux, please.
Waiter: Yes, monsieur—

Laszlo: I saw no one of Ugarte's description.
Ilsa: Victor! I, I feel, somehow, we shouldn't stay here.
Laszlo: If we would walk out so soon it would only call attention to us. Perhaps Ugarte's in some other part of the Cafe.

Berger: Excuse me, but, er, you look like a couple who are on the way to America.
Laszlo: Well?

Berger: You'll find a market there for this ring. I'm forced to sell it at a great sacrifice.
Laszlo: Thank you, but I hardly think—

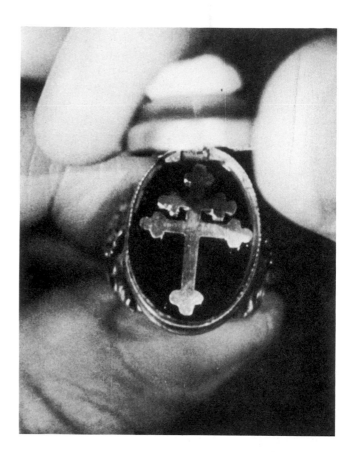

Berger: Then, perhaps, for the lady. The ring is quite unique.

Laszlo: Oh, yes. I'm very interested.
Berger: Good.

Laszlo: What is your name?
Berger: Berger. Norwegian. I'm at your service, sir.
Ilsa: Victor.
Laszlo: I'll meet you in a few minutes at the bar.

Laszlo: No. I don't think we want to buy the ring, but thank you for showing it to us.
Berger: Such a bargain. But that is your decision?
Laszlo: I'm sorry it is.

Renault: Monsieur Laszlo, is it not?
Laszlo: Yes.
Renault: I am Captain Renault, Prefect of Police.
Laszlo: Yes. What is it you want?

Renault: Merely to welcome you to Casablanca and to wish you a pleasant stay. It isn't often we have so distinguished a visitor.

Laszlo: Thank you. I hope you'll forgive me, Captain. The present French administration hasn't always been so cordial.

Laszlo: May I present Miss Ilsa Lund.

Renault: I was informed you were the most beautiful woman ever to visit Casablanca.

Renault: That was a gross understatement.
Ilsa: You're very kind.
Laszlo: Won't you join us?

Renault: Er, if you will permit me. Oh, no, Emile, please. A bottle of your best champagne. And put it on my bill.
Emile: Very well, sir.
Laszlo: Captain, please.

Renault: Oh, please, Monsieur. It is a little game we play. They put it on my bill. I tear up the bill. It is very convenient!

Ilsa: Captain, the boy who is playing the piano, somewhere I have seen him.
Renault: Sam?
Ilsa: Yes.

Renault: He came from Paris with Rick.
Ilsa: Rick? Who's he?
Renault: Mademoiselle, you are in Rick's and Rick is, er—
Ilsa: Is what?

Renault: Well, Mademoiselle, he's the kind of man that, well, if I were a woman, and I weren't around, I should be in love with Rick.

Renault: But what a fool I am, talking to a beautiful woman about another man. Er, excuse me.

Officer: Ah, Major!

Renault: Mademoiselle Lund and Monsieur Laszlo, may I present Major Heinrich Strasser.

Strasser: How do you do. This is a pleasure I've long looked forward to.
Laszlo: I'm sure you'll excuse me if I'm not gracious, but you see, I'm a Czechoslovakian.

Strasser: You *were* a Czechoslovakian. Now you are a subject of the German Reich!

Laszlo: I've never accepted that privilege, and I'm here now on French soil.

Strasser: I should like to discuss some matters arising from your presence on French soil.
Laszlo: This is hardly the time or the place.

Strasser: Then we shall state another time and another place. Tomorrow at ten in the Prefect's Office with Mademoiselle.

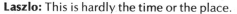

Laszlo: Captain Renault, I am under your authority. Is it your order, that we come to your office?
Renault: Er, let us say it is my request. That is a much more pleasant word.

Laszlo: Very well.
Renault: Mademoiselle.
Strasser: Mademoiselle.

Renault: A very clever, tactical retreat, Major.

Laszlo: This time they really mean to stop me.
Ilsa: Victor, I'm afraid for you.
Laszlo: We've been in difficult places before, haven't we?

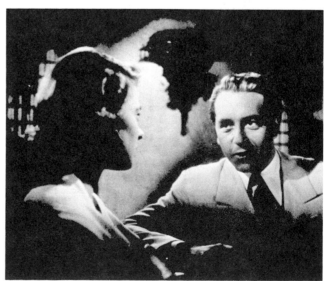

Laszlo: I must find out what Berger knows.
Ilsa: Be careful.
Laszlo: I will. Don't worry.

Laszlo: Mr. Berger, the ring. Could I see the ring?
Berger: Yes, Monsieur.
Laszlo: Champagne cocktail, please.

Berger: I recognize you from the news photographs, Monsieur Laszlo.
Laszlo: In a concentration camp, one is apt to lose a little weight.
Berger: We read five times that you were killed in five different places.
Laszlo: As you see, it was true every single time. Thank heaven I found you, Berger. I'm looking for a man by the name of Ugarte. He is supposed to help me.

Berger: Ugarte cannot even help himself, Monsieur. He is under arrest for murder. He was arrested here tonight.
Laszlo: I see.

88

Berger: But we who are still free will do all we can. We are organized, Monsieur. Underground like everywhere else. Tomorrow night there's a meeting at the Caverne du Roi. If you would come—

Ilsa: Will you ask the piano player to come over here, please?
Waiter: Very well, Mademoiselle.

Renault: How's the jewelry business, Berger?
Berger: Er, not so good. May I have my check, please?

Renault: Too bad you weren't here earlier, Monsieur Laszlo. We had quite a bit of excitement this evening. Didn't we, Berger?
Berger: Er, yes. Excuse me, gentlemen.

Laszlo: My bill.
Renault: No. Two champagne cocktails. Please.
Sacha: Yes, sir.

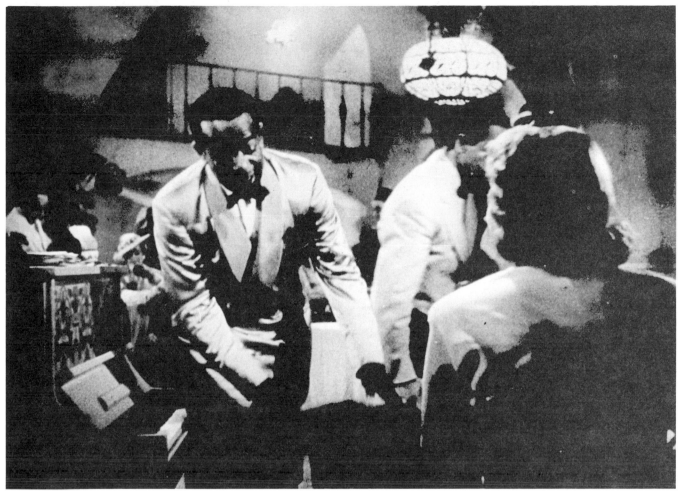

Ilsa: Hello, Sam.
Sam: Hello, Miss Ilsa. Ah never expected to see you again.

Ilsa: It's been a long time.
Sam: Yes, ma'am. A lot o' water under the bridge.

Ilsa: Some of the old songs, Sam.
Sam: Yes, ma'am.

Ilsa: Where is Rick?

Sam: Ah don't know. Ah ain't seen him all night.

Ilsa: When will he be back?
Sam: Not tonight no more. He ain't comin'. Er, he went home.

Ilsa: Does he always leave so early?
Sam: Oh he never—well, he's got a girl up at the Blue Parrot. Goes up there all the time.

Ilsa: You used to be a much better liar, Sam.

Sam: Leave him alone, Miss Ilsa. You're bad luck to him.

Ilsa: Play it once, Sam, for old time's sake.
Sam: Ah don't know what you mean, Miss Ilsa.

Ilsa: Play it, Sam.

Ilsa: Play, "As Time Goes By."

Sam: Oh, Ah can't remember it, Miss Ilsa. Ah'm a little rusty on it.
Ilsa: I'll hum it for you.

Ilsa: Hm-hm, hm-hm, hm-hmmm—

Ilsa: Sing it, Sam.

Sam: *"You must remember this;*
A kiss is just a kiss

A sigh is just a sigh

The fundamental things apply
As time goes by.

And when two lovers woo;
They still say 'I love you'

On that you can rely,
No matter what the future brings
As time goes by."

Rick: Sam, I thought I told you never to play it!

Renault: Well, you were asking about Rick and here he is!

Renault: Mademoiselle, may I present, er —

Rick: Hello, Ilsa.
Ilsa: Hello, Rick.
Renault: Oh, you've already met Rick, Mademoiselle?

Renault: Well, then, er, perhaps you also—
Ilsa: This is Mr. Laszlo.
Laszlo: How do you do?
Rick: How do you do?

Laszlo: One hears a great deal about Rick in Casablanca.

Rick: And about Victor Laszlo everywhere.

Laszlo: Won't you join us for a drink?
Renault: Oh, no, Rick, never—
Rick: Thanks, I will.

Renault: Well! A precedent is being broken.

Laszlo: This is a very interesting cafe. I congratulate you.
Rick: I congratulate you.
Laszlo: What for?

Rick: Your work.
Laszlo: Thank you. I try.
Rick: We *all* try. You succeed.

Renault: I can't get over you two. She was asking about you earlier, Rick, in a way that made me extremely jealous.

Ilsa: I wasn't sure you were the same. Let's see, the last time we met—

Rick: It was La Belle Aurore.

Ilsa: How nice. You remembered. But, of course, that was the day the Germans marched into Paris.
Rick: Not an easy day to forget.
Ilsa: No.

Rick: I remember every detail. The Germans wore gray; you wore blue.

Ilsa: Yes. I put that dress away. When the Germans march out I'll wear it again.

Renault: Ricky, you're becoming quite human. I suppose we have to thank you for that, Mademoiselle.

Laszlo: Ilsa, I don't wish to be the one to say it, but it's late.
Renault: So it is. And we have a curfew here in Casablanca. It would never do for the Chief of Police

Renault: to be found drinking after hours and have to fine himself.
Laszlo: I hope we didn't overstay our welcome.

Rick: Not at all.
Waiter: Your check, sir.
Rick: Oh, it's my party.
Renault: Another precedent gone. This has been a very interesting evening.

Renault: I'll call you a cab. Gasoline rationing, time of night.
Laszlo: We'll come again.
Rick: Any time.

Ilsa: Will you say good night to Sam for me?
Rick: I will.

Ilsa: There's still nobody in the world who can play "As Time Goes By" like Sam.

Rick: He hasn't played it in a long time.
Ilsa: Goodnight.

Laszlo: Goodnight.
Rick: Goodnight.

Laszlo: A very puzzling fellow, this Rick. What sort is he?
Ilsa: Oh, I really can't say, though I saw him quite often in Paris.

Renault: Tomorrow at ten at the Prefect's Office.
Laszlo: We'll be there.
Renault: Goodnight.

Ilsa: Goodnight.
Laszlo: Goodnight.

Sam: Boss! Boss!
Rick: Yeah?

Sam: Boss, ain't you goin' to bed?
Rick: Not right now.

Sam: Ain't you plannin' on goin' to bed in the near future?
Rick: No.

Sam: You evah goin' to bed?
Rick: No.
Sam: Well, I ain't sleepy, neither.
Rick: Good. Then have a drink.

Sam: No. Not me, boss.
Rick: Don't have a drink.

Sam: Boss, let's get out o' here.
Rick: No, sir. I'm waiting for a lady.

Sam: Please, boss, let's go. There ain't nuthin' but trouble for you here.
Rick: She's coming back. I know she's coming back.
Sam: We'll take the car and drive all night. We'll get drunk. We'll go fishin' and stay away until she's gone.

Rick: Shut up and go home, will you?
Sam: No, suh. Ah'm stayin' right here.

Rick: They grab Ugarte and then she walks in. Well, that's the way it goes. One in and one out. Sam—
Sam: Yes, boss?
Rick: If it's December 1941 in Casablanca, what time is it in New York?

Sam: What? My watch stopped.

Rick: I bet they're asleep in New York. I bet they're asleep all over America.

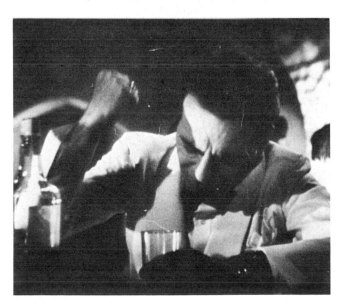 

Rick: Of all the gin joints in all the towns all over the world, she walks into mine.

Rick: What's that you're playing?
Sam: Oh, just a little somethin' of my own.

Rick: Well, stop it. You know what I want to hear.
Sam: No, I don't.

Rick: You played it for her. You can play it for me.
Sam: Well, I don't think I can remember it.
Rick: If she can stand it I can. Play it!
Sam: Yes, boss—

Rick: Who are you, really? And what were you before? What did you do and what did you think? Huh?

Ilsa: We said "no questions."

Rick: Here's looking at you, kid.

Ilsa: A franc for your thoughts.

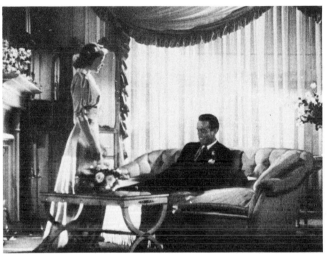

Rick: In America they'd bring only a penny. I guess that's about all they're worth.
Ilsa: Well, I'm willing to be overcharged. Tell me.
Rick: Well, I was wondering.

Ilsa: Yes?
Rick: Why I'm so lucky. Why I should find you waiting for me to come along.

Ilsa: Why there is no other man in my life.
Rick: Uh-huh.

Ilsa: That's easy. There was. And he's dead.

Rick: I'm sorry for asking. I forgot we said no questions.

Ilsa: Well, only one answer can take care of all our questions.

Rick: Nothing can stop them now! Wednesday, Thursday at the latest they'll be here in Paris!

Ilsa: Richard, they'll find out your record. It won't be safe for you here.

Rick: I'm on their blacklist already. Their roll of honor—

Sam: *"Moonlight and love songs never out of date*
Hearts full of passion, jealousy and hate!
Woman needs man and man must have his mate
That, no one can deny.

It's still the same old story,
A fight for love and glory—
A case of do or die
The world will always welcome lovers,

As time goes by."

Rick: Henri wants us to finish this bottle and then three more. He says he'll water his garden with champagne before he'll let the Germans drink it.

Sam: This ought to take the sting out o' bein' occupied. Doesn't it, Mr. Richard?

Rick: You said it.

Rick: Here's looking at you, kid.

Franzosen, Einwohner von Paris.

Franzosen, Einwohner von Paris.

Hört aufmerksam zu.
Die deutschen Truppen stehen vor den Toren von Paris.

Euer Aufstand ist ohne jegliche Verteidigung, eure Ehre ist in Auflosung begriffen.

Seid unbesorgt, wir werden Ruhe und Ordnung wieder herstellen.

Rick: My German's a little rusty.

Ilsa: It's the gestapo! They say they expect to be in Paris tomorrow.

Ilsa: They're telling us how to act when they come marching in.

Ilsa: With the whole world crumbling we pick this time to fall in love.

Rick: Yeah, it's pretty bad timing. Where were you, say, ten years ago?

Ilsa: Ten years ago? Let's see. Yes. I was having a brace put on my teeth. Where were you?

Rick: Looking for a job.

Ilsa: Was that cannon fire?

Ilsa: Or was it my heart pounding?

Rick: It's the new German 77. But if judging by the sound, only about 35 miles away.

Rick: And getting closer every minute.

Rick: Here. Here. Drink up. We'll never finish the other three

Sam: The Germans'll be here pretty soon now and they'll come looking for you. And don't forget, there's a price on your head.

Rick: And I left a note in my apartment. They'll know where to find me.

Ilsa: Oh, it's strange. I know so very little about you.

Rick: I know very little about you. Just the fact that you had your teeth straightened.

Ilsa: But be serious, darling. You are in danger. You must leave Paris.

Rick: No, no, no. *We* must leave . . .

Ilsa: Yes, of course. *We . . .*

Rick: Well, the train for Marseilles leaves at five o'clock. I'll pick you up at your hotel at four-thirty.

Ilsa: No, no, not my hotel. I, I have things to do in the city before I leave. I'll meet you at the station.

Rick: All right. At a quarter to five. Say, why don't we get married in Marseilles?

Ilsa: Well, I—that's a little too far ahead to plan—
Rick: Yes, I guess it is a little too far ahead. Well, let's see. Er, what about the engineer? Why can't he marry us on the train?

Ilsa: Oh, darling—
Rick: Well, why not? The captain on a ship can. It doesn't seem fair that

Rick: Hey! Hey, what's wrong, kid?

Ilsa: I love you so much.

Ilsa: And I hate this war so much. Oh, it's a crazy world. Anything can happen.

Ilsa: If you shouldn't get away, I mean, if, if something should happen to keep us apart.

Ilsa: Wherever they put you and wherever I'll be,

Ilsa: I want you to know that I —

Ilsa: Kiss me! Kiss me as though it were the last time!

Announcer: Le dernier train part en trois minutes!

Rick: Where is she? Have you seen her?

Sam: No, Mr. Richard. I can't find her. She checked out of the hotel.

Sam: But this note came just after you left.

Sam: That's the last call, Mr. Richard. Do you hear me? Come on, Mr. Richard. Let's get out o' here. Come on Mr. Richard. Come on!

Announcer: En voiture!

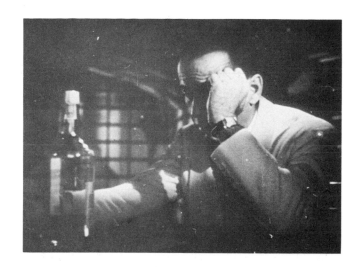 

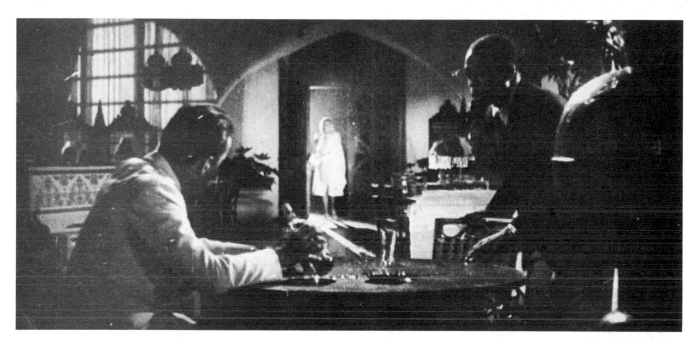

Ilsa: Rick, I have to talk to you.
Rick: Oh. I saved my first drink to have with you. Here.

Ilsa: No. No, Rick, not tonight.
Rick: Especially tonight.
Ilsa: Please don't.

Rick: Why did you have to come to Casablanca? There're other places.

Ilsa: I wouldn't have come if I'd known that you were here. Believe me, Rick, it's true, I didn't know.

Rick: Funny about your voice, how it hasn't changed. I can still hear it. "Richard dear, I'll go with you anyplace. We'll get on a train together and we'll never stop."
Ilsa: Please don't. Don't, Rick! I can understand how you feel.

Rick: You understand how I feel. How long was it we had, honey?
Ilsa: I didn't count the days.
Rick: Well, I did. Every one of them.

136

Rick: Mostly I remember the last one.

Rick: A wow finish. A guy standing on a station platform in the rain. With a comical look on his face, because his insides had been kicked out.

Ilsa: Can I tell you a story, Rick?
Rick: Has it got a wow finish?
Ilsa: I don't know the finish yet.

Rick: Well, go on, tell it. Maybe one'll come to you as you go along.
Ilsa: It's about a girl who had just come to Paris from her home in Oslo. At the house of some friends she met a man, about whom she'd heard her whole life.

Ilsa: A very great and courageous man. He opened up for her a whole beautiful world full of knowledge and thoughts and ideals. Everything she knew or ever became was because of him. And she looked up to him, worshipped him with a feeling she supposed was love. 137

Rick: Yes, that's very pretty. I heard a story once. As a matter of fact, I've heard a lot of stories in my time.

Rick: They went along with the sound of a tinny piano, playing in the parlor downstairs.

Rick: "Mister, I met a man once when I was a kid," they'd always begin.

Rick: Well, I guess neither one of our stories was very funny.

138

Rick: Tell me, who was it you left me for? Was it Laszlo or were there others in between? Or aren't you the kind that tells?

  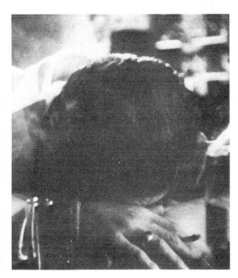

Strasser: I strongly suspect that Ugarte left the Letters of Transit with Mr. Blaine. I would suggest you search the Cafe immediately and thoroughly.
Renault: If Rick has the Letters, he's much too smart to let you find them there.

Strasser: You give him credit for too much cleverness. My impression was that he's just another blundering American.

Renault: Well we mustn't underestimate American blundering. I was with them when they blundered into Berlin in 1918.

Strasser: As to Laszlo, we want him watched twenty-four hours a day.
Renault: It may interest you to know that at this very moment he's on his way here.

Officer: There's nothing we can do.

Renault: I'm delighted to see you both. Did you have a good night's rest?
Laszlo: I slept very well.
Renault: That's strange. Nobody's supposed to sleep well in Casablanca.

Laszlo: May we proceed with the business?
Renault: With pleasure. Won't you sit down?
Laszlo: Thank you.

Strasser: Very well, Herr Laszlo, we will not mince words. You are an escaped prisoner of the Reich. So far you have been fortunate enough to elude us. You have reached Casablanca. It is my duty to see that you stay in Casablanca.

Laszlo: Whether or not you'll succeed is, of course, problematical.
Strasser: Not at all. Captain Renault's signature is necessary on every exit visa.

Strasser: Captain, would you think it is possible that Herr Laszlo will receive a visa?

Renault: I'm afraid not. My regrets, Monsieur.

Laszlo: Well, perhaps I shall like it in Casablanca.
Strasser: And Mademoiselle?
Ilsa: You needn't be concerned about me.

Laszlo: Is that all you wish to tell us?

Strasser: Don't be in such a hurry.

Strasser: You have all the time in the world. You may be in Casablanca indefinitely.

Strasser: Or you may leave for Lisbon tomorrow. On one condition.

Laszlo: And that is?
Strasser: You know the leaders of the Underground Movement in Paris, in Prague, in Brussels, in Amsterdam, in Oslo, in Belgrade, in Athens—
Laszlo: Even Berlin.

Strasser: Yes, even in Berlin. If you will furnish me with their names and their whereabouts, you will have your visa in the morning.

Renault: And the honor of having served the Third Reich.
Laszlo: I was in a German concentration camp for a year. That's honor enough for a lifetime.

Strasser: You will give us the names?
Laszlo: If I didn't give them to you in a concentration camp I certainly won't give them to you now.

Laszlo: And what if you track down these men and kill them? What if you murdered all of us? From every corner of Europe hundreds, thousands, would rise to take our places. Even Nazis can't kill that fast.

Strasser: Herr Laszlo, you have a reputation for eloquence which I can now understand. But in one respect you are mistaken. You said the enemies of the Reich could all be replaced. But there is one exception, no one could take your place in the event anything unfortunate should occur to you while you were trying to escape.

Laszlo: You won't dare to interfere with me here. This is still unoccupied France. Any violation of neutrality would reflect on Captain Renault.

Renault: Monsieur, insofar as it is in my power.
Laszlo: Thank you.

Renault: Er, by the way, Monsieur, last night you evinced an interest in Signor Ugarte.
Laszlo: Yes?

Renault: I believe you have a message for him.

Laszlo: Nothing important, but may I speak to him now?

144

Strasser: You would find the conversation a trifle one-sided. Signor Ugarte's dead.

Renault: I'm making out the report now.

Renault: We haven't quite decided whether he committed suicide or died trying to escape.

Laszlo: Are you quite finished with us?
Strasser: For the time being.

Laszlo: Good day.

Renault: Undoubtedly their next step will be the Black Market.

Officer: Excuse me, Captain. Another visa problem has come up.
Renault: Show her in.
Officer: Yes, Monsieur.

145

Native: I'm sorry, Monsieur, we would have to handle the police. This is a job for Signor Ferrari.
Man: Ferrari?
Native: It can be most helpful to know Signor Ferrari. He's pretty near got a monopoly on the Black Market here.

Native: You will find him over there at the Blue Parrot.
Man: Thanks.

Ferrari: There, don't be too downhearted. Perhaps you can come to terms with Captain Renault.
Jan: Thank you very much, Signor.

Rick: Hello, Ferrari.
Ferrari: Ah, good morning, Rick!

Rick: I see the bus is in. I'll take my shipment with me.

Ferrari: No hurry. I'll have it sent over.

Ferrari: Have a drink with me.
Rick: I never drink in the morning. And every time you send my shipment over, it's always just a little bit short.
Ferrari: Carrying charges, my boy, carrying charges.

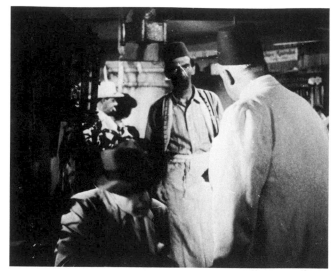

Ferrari: Here, sit down. There's something I want to talk over with you, anyhow. The Bourbon.

Ferrari: Ah. The news about Ugarte upsets me very much.
Rick: You're a fat hypocrite. You don't feel any sorrier for Ugarte than I do.

Ferrari: Of course not. What upsets me is the fact that Ugarte is dead and no one knows where those Letters of Transit are.

Rick: Practically no one.

Ferrari: If I could lay my hands on those Letters, I could make a fortune.
Rick: Oh, so could I. And I'm a poor business man.

Ferrari: I have a proposition for whoever has those Letters. I'll handle the entire transaction, get rid of the Letters, take all the risk, for a small percentage.

Rick: And the carrying charges?

Ferrari: Naturally there'll be a few incidental expenses. That's the proposition I have for whoever has those Letters.

Rick: I'll tell him when he comes in.

Ferrari: Rick, I'll put my cards on the table. I think you know where those Letters are.
Rick: Well, you're in good company. Renault and Strasser probably think so too. That's why I came over here to give them a chance to ransack my place.

Ferrari: Rick, don't be a fool. Take me into your confidence. You need a partner.
Rick: Excuse me. I'll be getting back.

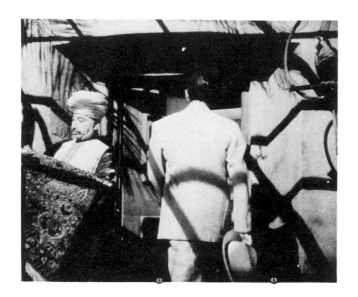

Laszlo: Good morning.
Rick: Signor Ferrari is the fat gent at the table.

Dealer: You will not find a treasure like this in all Morocco, Mademoiselle. Only 700 francs.

Rick: You're being cheated.
Ilsa: It doesn't matter, thank you.
Dealer: Ah, the lady is a friend of Rick's? For friends of Rick's we have a small discount. Did I say 700 francs?

Dealer: You can have it for 200.
Rick: I'm sorry I was in no condition to receive you when you called on me last night.
Ilsa: It doesn't matter.

Dealer: Er, for special friends of Rick's we have a special discount. 100 francs.
Rick: Your story had me a little confused. Or maybe it was the Bourbon.

Dealer: I have some tablecloths, some napkins —

Ilsa: Thank you. I'm really not interested.
Dealer: Please, one minute. Please.

Rick: Why did you come back?

Rick: To tell me why you ran out on me at the railway station?
Ilsa: Yes.

Rick: Well, you can tell me now. I'm reasonably sober.

Ilsa: I don't think I will, Rick.
Rick: Why not? After all, I got stuck with a railway ticket. I think I'm entitled to know.

Ilsa: Last night I saw what has happened to you.

Ilsa: The Rick I knew in Paris, I could tell him. He'd understand. But the one who looked at me with such hatred.

Ilsa: I'll be leaving Casablanca soon and we'll never see each other again. We knew very little about each other when we were in love in Paris. If we leave it that way maybe we'll remember those days, not Casablanca, not last night.

Rick: Did you run out on me because you couldn't take it? Because you knew what it would be like, hiding from the police, running away all the time?
Ilsa: You can believe that if you want to.

Rick: Well, I'm not running away anymore. I'm settled now, above a saloon, it's true. But—walk up a flight, I'll be expecting you.

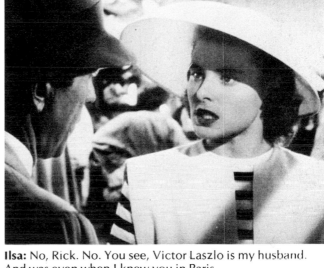

Rick: Well, all the same, someday you'll lie to Laszlo—you'll be there.

Ilsa: No, Rick. No. You see, Victor Laszlo is my husband. And was even when I knew you in Paris.

Ferrari: I was just telling Monsieur Laszlo that unfortunately I am not able to help him.
Ilsa: Oh.

Laszlo: You see, my dear. The word has gone around.
Ferrari: As leader of all illegal activities in Casablanca, I'm an influential and respected man.

Ferrari: It would not be worth my life to do anything for Monsieur Laszlo. You, however, are a different matter.

Laszlo: Er, Signor Ferrari thinks it might just be possible to get an exit visa for you.

Ilsa: You mean for me to go on alone?
Ferrari: And only alone.

Laszlo: I will stay here and keep on trying. I'm sure that in a little while—

Ferrari: We might as well be frank, Monsieur. It'll take a miracle to get you out of Casablanca. And the Germans have outlawed miracles.

Ilsa: We are only interested in two visas, Signor.
Laszlo: Please, Ilsa. Don't be hasty.
Ilsa: No, Victor. No.

Ferrari: You two will want to discuss this. Excuse me. I'll be at the bar.

Laszlo: No, Ilsa. I won't let you stay here. You must get to America. And, believe me, somehow I'll get out and join you.

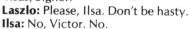

Ilsa: But, Victor, if the situation were different. If I had to stay and there was only a visa for one, would you take it?

Laszlo: Yes, I would.
Ilsa: Yes, I see. When I had trouble getting out of Lille, why didn't you leave me there? And when I was sick in Marseilles, and held you up for two weeks and you were in danger every minute of the time, why didn't you leave me then?

Laszlo: I meant to. But something always held me up. I love you very much, Ilsa.

Ilsa: Your secret will be safe with me. Ferrari is waiting for our answer.

Ferrari: Not more than 50 francs, though!

Laszlo: We've decided, Signor Ferrari. For the present we'll go on looking for *two* visas. Thank you very much.
Ferrari: Well. Good luck. But be careful. You know that you're being shadowed?
Laszlo: Of course, it becomes an instinct.

Ferrari: I observe that you, in one respect, are a very fortunate man, monsieur. I'm moved to make one more suggestion.

156

Ferrari: Why, I do not know, because it cannot possibly profit me. But have you heard about Signor Ugarte and the Letters of Transit?
Laszlo: Yes, something.

Ferrari: Those letters were not found on Ugarte when they arrested him.
Laszlo: Do you know where they are?
Ferrari: Not for sure, monsieur. But I'll venture to guess that Ugarte left those letters with Monsieur Rick.

Laszlo: Rick?

Ferrari: He is a difficult customer that Rick. One never knows what he'll do or why. But it is worth a chance.
Laszlo: Thank you very much. Good day.

Ilsa: Goodbye. Thank you for your coffee, Signor. I shall miss that when we leave Casablanca.
Ferrari: It was gracious of you to share it with me. Good day, Mademoiselle. Monsieur.
Laszlo: Good day.

Foreigner: Here's to you, sir.
Tourist: Er, good luck. Yeh—
Foreigner: I'd better be going.
Tourist: Er, my check, please.

Foreigner: I have to warn you, sir. I beseech you—
Tourist: Yeh—

158

Foreigner: This is a dangerous place full of vultures. Vultures everywhere!
Tourist: Yeh—

Foreigner: Thanks for everything.
Tourist: Er, goodbye, sir.
Foreigner: It has been a pleasure to meet you.

Foreigner: Oh. I'm sorry.

Carl: Monsieur Rick. You are getting to be your best customer.

Renault: Well, Ricky. I'm very pleased with you. Now you're beginning to live like a Frenchman.
Rick: That was some going over your men gave my place this afternoon. We just barely got cleaned up in time to open.
Renault: Well, I told Strasser he wouldn't find the letters here. But I told my men to be especially destructive.

Renault: You know how that impresses Germans. Rick, have you got those Letters of Transit?
Rick: Louis! Are you Pro-Vichy or Free French?
Renault: Serves me right for asking a direct question. The subject is closed.

Rick: Well, it looks like you're a little late.
Renault: Huh?

Rick: So Yvonne's gone over to the enemy?

Renault: Who knows? In her own way, she may constitute an entire second front. Well, I think it's time for me to flatter Major Strasser a little. I'll see you later, Rick.

Yvonne: Sacha!
German: French 75's.

Yvonne: Put up a whole row of them, Sacha, starting here and ending here.
German: We will begin with two.

French Officier: Dites, vous. Vous n'êtes donc pas française pour aller comme ça avec des Allemands!
Yvonne: De quoi vous mêlez-vous?

Officier: Je me mêle—
Yvonne: Ça ne vous regarde pas.

German: No, no, no, no. What did you say? Would you kindly repeat it?

French: What I said is none of your business.

German: I will make it my business.

Yvonne: Arrêtez! Je vous en prie! Je vous en prie! Arrêtez!

Rick: I don't like disturbances in my place.

Rick: Either lay off politics or get out!

Officier: Sale boche. Le jour de notre vengeance viendra!

Strasser: You see, captain, the situation is not as much under control as you believe.

Renault: My dear major, we are trying to cooperate with your government. But we cannot regulate the feelings of our people.
Strasser: Captain, are you entirely certain which side you're on?

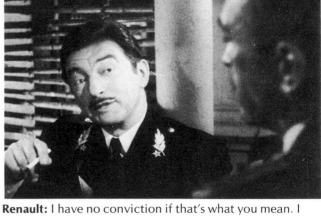

Renault: I have no conviction if that's what you mean. I blow with the wind. And the prevailing wind happens to be from Vichy.
Strasser: And if it should change?
Renault: Oh, surely the Reich doesn't admit that possibility.

Strasser: We are concerned about more than Casablanca. We know that every French province in Africa is honeycombed with traitors waiting for their chance, waiting, perhaps, for a leader.

Renault: A leader? Like Laszlo?
Strasser: I have been thinking. It is too dangerous if we let him go. It may be too dangerous if we let him stay.
Renault: I can see what you mean.

Carl: Da bin ich wieder, Leuchtag. Ich habe Ihnen den besten Cognac gebracht.
Mr. Leuchtag: Danke, Carl.

Carl: Für Frau Leuchtag.
Mrs. Leuchtag: Danke, Carl.
Carl: Herr Leuchtag!

Mr. Leuchtag: Tausend Dank. Sit down, Carl. Have a brandy with us.
Mrs. Leuchtag: To celebrate our leaving for America tomorrow.

Carl: Oh thank you very much. I thought you would ask, so I brought the good brandy. And the glass.
Mrs. Leuchtag: At last the day has come!

Mr. Leuchtag: Frau Leuchtag and I are speaking nothing but English now.
Mrs. Leuchtag: So we should feel at home when we get to America.
Carl: A very nice idea.

Mr. Leuchtag: To America!
Mrs. Leuchtag: To America!
Carl: To America!

Mr. Leuchtag: My dear, what watch?
Mrs. Leuchtag: Ten watch.
Mr. Leuchtag: Such much?

Carl: Er, you will get along beautifully in America.

Renault: How's lady luck treating you? Too bad. You'll find him over there.

Rick: Yes?
Annina: Could I speak to you for just a moment please?
Rick: How did you get in here? You're under age.

Annina: I came with Captain Renault.
Rick: I should have known.
Annina: My husband is with me, too.

Rick: He is? Captain Renault's getting broadminded. Sit down. Will you have a drink?
Annina: No, thank you.
Rick: Of course not. Do you mind if I do?

Annina: No. Monsieur Rick. What kind of a man is Captain Renault?
Rick: Oh, he's just like any other man only more so.
Annina: I mean, i-is he trustworthy? Is his word—

166

Rick: Now, just a minute. Who told you to ask me that?
Annina: He did. Captain Renault did.
Rick: I thought so. Where's your husband?
Annina: At the roulette table. Trying to win enough for our exit visas. Oh, of course he's losing.

Rick: How long have you been married?
Annina: Eight weeks. We come from Bulgaria. Oh, things are very bad there, monsieur. The devil has the people by the throat. So Jan and I, we—We do not want our children to grow up in such a country.
Rick: Er, so you decided to go to America?

Annina: Yes. But we have not much money and travelling is so expensive and difficult. It was much more than we thought to get here. And then Captain Renault sees us and he is so kind. He wants to help us.
Rick: Yes. I'll bet.

Annina: He tells me he can give us an exit visa. But, but we have no money.

Rick: Does he know that?
Annina: Oh, yes.
Rick: And he's still willing to give you a visa?

Annina: Yes, monsieur.

Rick: And you want to know—

Annina: Will he keep his word?

Rick: He always has.

Annina: Oh, monsieur. You are a man.

Annina: If someone loved you very much, so that your happiness was the only thing that she wanted in the world and she did a bad thing to make certain of it, could you forgive her?

Rick: Nobody ever loved me that much.

Annina: And he never knew. And the girl kept this bad thing locked in her heart. That would be all right, wouldn't it?

Rick: You want my advice?
Annina: Oh, yes, please.
Rick: Go back to Bulgaria.

Annina: Oh, b-but if you knew what it means to us to leave Europe, to get to America—Oh, but if Jan should find out. He is such a boy. In many ways I, I am so much older than he is.

Rick: Yes. Well, everybody in Casablanca has problems. Yours may work out. You'll excuse me?

Annina: Thank you, Monsieur.

Rick: Good evening.
Laszlo: Good evening. You see, here we are again.

Rick: I take that as a great compliment to Sam. I suppose he means to you, Paris, well, of happier days.

Ilsa: He does. Could we have a table close to him?
Laszlo: And as far away from Major Strasser as possible.

Rick: Well, the geography may be a little difficult to arrange. Paul! Table 30!

Paul: Yes, sir. Right this way, if you please.

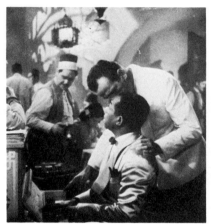

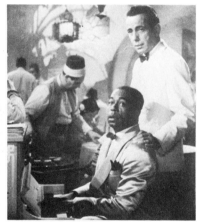

Rick: I'll have Sam play "As Time Goes By." I believe that's your favorite tune.
Ilsa: Thank you.

Laszlo: Two cognacs, please.
Waiter: Cognacs!

Croupier: Faites vos jeux, mesdames et messieurs. Les jeux sont faits! La boule passe! Les jeux sont faits! Le numéro 8! Tout est payé au numéro!

Rick: Have you tried 22 tonight?
Jan: No. No. I, I guess not.

Rick: I said 22.

Croupier: Faites vos jeux, mesdames et messieurs.

Croupier: Les jeux sont faits! Rien ne va plus!

Croupier: Pair et passe. Le numéro 22!

Rick: Leave it there.

Croupier: Faites vos jeux, mesdames et messieurs! La boule passe. Faites vos jeux.

Croupier: Les jeux sont faits. Rien ne va plus!

Croupier: 22!

Rick: Cash it in and don't come back.

Customer: Say, are you sure this place is honest?
Carl: Honest? As honest as the day is long.

Croupier: Bets are closed!
Rick: How we doin' tonight?
Croupier: Well, a couple of thousand less than I thought there would be.

Annina: Monsieur Rick, I—

Rick: He's just a lucky guy.

Carl: Monsieur Rick, may I get you a cup of coffee?
Rick: No, thanks, Carl.

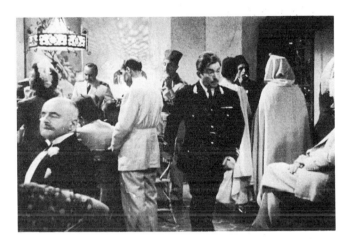

Jan: Captain Renault, may I—
Renault: Oh, not yet, please. Come to my office in the morning. We'll do everything business like.
Jan: We'll be there at six.

Renault: I'll be there at ten. I'm very happy for both of you. Still it's very strange that you won. Well, maybe not so strange. I'll see you in the morning.
Annina: Thank you so much, Captain Renault.

175

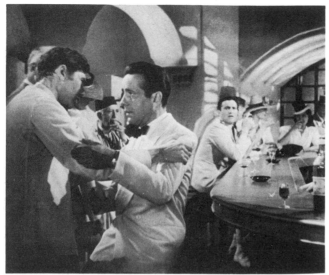

Sacha: Boss, you've done a beautiful thing.

Rick: Go away, you crazy Russian!

Renault: As I suspected, you're a rank sentimentalist!
Rick: Yeah? Why?
Renault: Why do you interfere with my little romance.

Rick: Put it down as a gesture to love.
Renault: Well, I forgive you this time. But I'll be in tomorrow night with a breath-taking blonde. And it will make me very happy if she loses.

Laszlo: Monsieur Blaine, I wonder if I could talk to you.
Rick: Go ahead.
Laszlo: Well, isn't there some other place? This is rather confidential what I have to say.

Rick: To my office.

Laszlo: Right. You must know it's very important that I get out of Casablanca. It's my privilege to be one of the leaders of the great movement.

Laszlo: You know what I have been doing.

Laszlo: You know what it means to the work, to the lives of thousands and thousands of people that I be free to reach America and **continue my** work.

177

Rick: I'm not interested in politics. The problems of the world are not in my department. I'm a saloon-keeper.

Laszlo: My friends in the Underground tell me that you've quite a record. You ran guns to Ethiopia. You fought against the Fascists in Spain.

Rick: What of it?

Laszlo: Isn't it strange that you always happened to be fighting on the side of the under-dog?

Rick: Yes. I found that a **very** expensive hobby, too. But then I never was much of a business man.

Laszlo: Are you enough of a business man to appreciate an offer of a hundred thousand francs?

Rick: I appreciate it, but I don't accept it.
Laszlo: I'll raise it to two hundred thousand.

Rick: My friend, you can make it a million francs, or three, my answer would still be the same.

Laszlo: There must be some reason why you won't let me have them.

Rick: There is. I suggest that you ask your wife.
Laszlo: I beg your pardon?

Rick: I said, ask your wife.
Laszlo: My wife!
Rick: Yes.

Germans: Es braust ein Ruf wie Donnerhall,

wie Schwertgeklirr und Wogenprall:

zum Rhein, zum Rhein, zum deutschen Rhein!
Wer will des Stromes Hüter sein!

Lieb Vaterland, magst ruhig sein,

lieb Vaterland, magst ruhig sein,

fest steht und treu die Wacht,

die Wacht am Rhein, fest steht und treu

die Wacht, die Wacht am Rhein!

Lieb Vaterland, magst ruhig sein
Laszlo: Play "La Marseillaise!" Play it!

lieb Vaterland,

magst ruhig sein,
Laszlo: *Allons, enfants de la Patrie,*

181

fest steht und treu die Wacht,
Le jour de gloire est arrive!
Contre nous de la tyrannie

die Wacht am Rhein,

fest steht und treu
L'étendard sanglant est levé, L'étendard sanglant est levé!

die Wacht, die **W***acht . . .*

Entendez-vous dans les campagnes

Mugir ces féroces soldats?

Ils viennent jusque dans nos bras
Esgorger nos fils, nos campagnes.

Aux armes, citoyens!
Formez vos bataillons!

Marchons,

marchons!

Qu'un sang impur

Abreuve nos sillons!

Yvonne: Vive la France! Vive la Democratie!

Strasser: You see what I mean? If Laszlo's presence in a cafe can inspire this unfortunate demonstration, what more will his presence in Casablanca bring on? I advise that this place be shut up at once!

Renault: But everybody's having such a good time.
Strasser: Yes. Much too good a time. The place is to be closed.
Renault: But I have no excuse to close it.
Strasser: Find one.

Renault: Everybody is to leave here immediately! This cafe is closed until further notice!

Renault: Clear the room at once!

Rick: How can you close me up? On what grounds?
Renault: I'm shocked! Shocked to find that gambling is going on here!

Croupier: Your winnings, sir.
Renault: Oh, thank you very much.

Renault: Everybody out at once!

186

Strasser: Mademoiselle, after this disturbance it is not safe for Laszlo to stay in Casablanca.
Ilsa: This morning you implied it was not safe for him to leave Casablanca.

Strasser: That is also true. Except for one destination. To return to Occupied France.
Ilsa: Occupied France?
Strasser: Under a safe conduct from me.

Ilsa: What value is that? You may recall what German guarantees have been worth in the past.
Strasser: There are only two other alternatives for him.
Ilsa: What are they?

Strasser: It is possible the French authorities will find a reason to put him in the concentration camp here.
Ilsa: And the other alternative?
Strasser: My dear Mademoiselle, perhaps you have already observed that in Casablanca human life is cheap. Good night, Mademoiselle.

Ilsa: What happened with Rick?

Laszlo: We'll discuss it later.

Laszlo: Our faithful friend is still there.

Ilsa: Victor, please don't go to the Underground meeting tonight.

Laszlo: I must. Besides, it isn't often that a man has the chance to display heroics before his wife.
Ilsa: Don't joke. After Major Strasser's warning tonight, I'm frightened.

Laszlo: To tell you the truth, I'm frightened, too. Shall I remain here in the hotel room hiding, or shall I carry on the best I can?
Ilsa: Whatever I'd say, you'd carry on. Victor, why don't you tell me about Rick? What did you find out?

Laszlo: Apparently he has the letters.
Ilsa: Yes?
Laszlo: But no intention of selling them. One would think if sentiment wouldn't persuade him, money would.

Ilsa: Did he give any reason?

Laszlo: He suggested I ask you.

Ilsa: Ask me?
Laszlo: Yes, he said, "Ask your wife."
I don't know why he said that.

Laszlo: Well, our friend outside will think we've retired by now. I'll be going in a few minutes.

Laszlo: Ilsa, I—
Ilsa: Yes?

Laszlo: When I was in the concentration camp, were you lonely in Paris?
Ilsa: Yes, Victor, I was.

Laszło: I know how it is to be lonely. Is there anything you wish to tell me?

Ilsa: No, Victor, there isn't.

Laszlo: I love you very much my dear.

Ilsa: Yes. Yes, I know. Victor, **whatever I do**, will you **believe that I, that I —**

Laszlo: You don't even have to say it. I'll believe.
Goodnight, dear.
Ilsa: Goodnight.

Ilsa: Victor!

Laszlo: Yes, dear?
Ilsa: Be careful.
Laszlo: Of course, I'll be careful.

Carl: Well, you are in pretty good shape, Herr Rick.

Rick: How long can I afford to stay closed?
Carl: Oh, two weeks, maybe three.

Rick: Maybe I won't have to. A bribe has worked before. In the meantime, everybody stays on salary.

Carl: Oh, thank you, Herr Rick. Sacha will be happy to hear it. I owe him **money**.

Rick: Now you finish locking up, will you, Carl?
Carl: I will. Then I am going to the meeting of the—

Rick: Don't tell me where you're going.
Carl: I won't.

Rick: Good night.
Carl: Good night, Monsieur Rick.

Rick: How did you get in?
Ilsa: The stairs from the street.

Rick: I told you this morning you'd come **around**, but this is a little ahead of schedule. Well, **won't you sit** down?

Ilsa: Richard, I had to see you.

Rick: So it's Richard again! We're back in Paris.
Ilsa: Please.
Rick: Your unexpected visit isn't connected by any chance with the Letters of Transit? It seems as long as I have those letters I'll never be lonely.

Ilsa: You can ask any price you want, but you must give me those letters.
Rick: I went all through that with your husband. It's no deal.
Ilsa: Well, I know how you feel about me, but I'm asking you to put your feelings aside for something more important.

Rick: Do I have to hear again what a great man your husband is? What an important Cause he's fighting for?
Ilsa: It was your Cause, too. In your own way; you were fighting for the same thing.

Rick: I'm not fighting for anything anymore, except myself. I'm the only cause I'm interested in.

Ilsa: Richard, we loved each other once. If those days meant anything at all to you—
Rick: I wouldn't bring up Paris if I were you. It's poor salesmanship.

Ilsa: Please. Please listen to me. If you knew what really happened. If you only knew the truth.
Rick: I wouldn't believe you no matter what you told me. You'd say anything to get what you want.

Ilsa: You want to feel sorry for yourself, don't you?

Ilsa: With so much at stake, all you can think of is your own feeling.

Ilsa: One woman has hurt you, and you take your revenge on the rest of the world. You're—you're a coward and a weakling!

Ilsa: No. Oh, Richard, I'm sorry. I'm sorry but, but you, you are our last hope. If you don't help us Victor Laszlo will die in Casablanca.

Rick: What of it? I'm going to die in Casablanca.

Rick: It's a good spot for it.

Rick: Now if you—

Ilsa: All right. I tried to reason with you. I tried everything. Now I want those letters. Get them for me!

Rick: I don't have to. I got them right here.

Ilsa: Put them on the table.

Rick: No.

Ilsa: For the last time, put them on the table.

Rick: If Laszlo and the Cause mean so much to you, you won't stop at anything.

Rick: All right, I'll make it easier for you.

Rick: Go ahead and shoot. You'll be doing me a favor.

Ilsa: Richard, I tried to stay away.
I thought I would never see you again.
That you were out of my life.

Ilsa: The day you left Paris, if you knew what I went through.

Ilsa: If you knew how much I loved you, how much I still love you.

Rick: And then?

Ilsa: It wasn't long after we were married that Victor went back to Czechoslovakia. They needed him in Prague, but there the Gestapo were waiting for him.

Ilsa: Just a two line item in the paper: "Victor Laszlo apprehended. Sent to concentration camp." I was frantic. For months, I tried to get word. Then it came.

Ilsa: He was dead, shot, trying to escape. I was lonely. I had nothing. Not even hope. Then I met you.

Rick: Why weren't you honest with me? Why did you keep your marriage a secret?

Ilsa: Oh, it wasn't my secret, Richard.

Ilsa: Victor wanted it that way. Not even our closest friends knew about our marriage. That was his way of protecting me.

Ilsa: I knew so much about his work, and if the Gestapo found out I was his wife it would be dangerous for me and for those working with us.

Rick: Well, when did you first find out he was alive?

Ilsa: Just before you and I were to leave Paris together. A friend came and told me that Victor was alive. They were hiding him in a freight car on the outskirts of Paris.

Ilsa: He was sick; he needed me. I wanted to tell you but I, I didn't dare. I knew, I knew you wouldn't have left Paris, and the Gestapo would have caught you.

Ilsa: So I—Well, well, you know the rest.

Rick: But it's still a story without an ending.

Rick: What about now?

Ilsa: Now? I don't know. I know that I'll never have the strength to leave you again.

Rick: And Laszlo?

Ilsa: You'll help him now, Richard, won't you? You'll see that he gets out?

Ilsa: And then he'll have his work. All that he's been living for.

Rick: All except one. He won't have you.

Ilsa: I can't fight it anymore. I ran away from you once. can't do it again.

Ilsa: Oh, I don't know what's right any longer.

Ilsa: You'll have to think for both of us, for all of us.

Rick: All right, I will.

Rick: Here's looking at you, kid.

Ilsa: I wish I didn't love you so much.

Carl: I think we lost them.
Laszlo: Yes. I'm afraid they caught some of the others.

Carl: Come inside. Come. I will help you. Come in here.
Laszlo: Thank you.

Carl: I will get you some water.

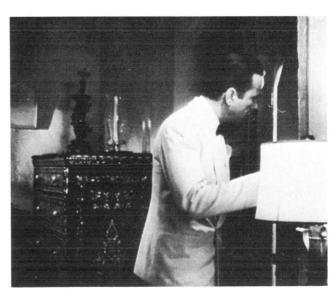

Rick: Carl, what happened?
Carl: The police break up our meeting, Herr Rick. We escaped in the last moment.
Rick: Come up here a minute.

Carl: Yes, I come.
Rick: I want you to turn out the light in the rear entrance. It might attract the police.
Carl: But Sacha always puts out the light.

Rick: Tonight he forgot!

Carl: Yes, I come. I will do it.

Rick: I want you to take Miss Lund home.
Carl: Yes, Herr Rick.

209

Laszlo: It's nothing. Just a little cut. We had to get through a window.

Rick: Oh. This might come in handy.
Laszlo: Thank you.
Rick: Had a close one, eh?
Laszlo: Yes, rather.

Rick: Don't you sometimes wonder if it's worth all this? I mean what you're fighting for.

Laszlo: We might as well question why we breathe. If we stop breathing, we'll die. If we stop fighting our enemies, the world will die.

Rick: What of it? Then it'll be out of its misery.

Laszlo: Do you know how you **sound**, Monsieur Blaine? Like a man who's trying to convince himself of something he doesn't believe in his heart.

Laszlo: Each of us has a destiny. For good or evil.

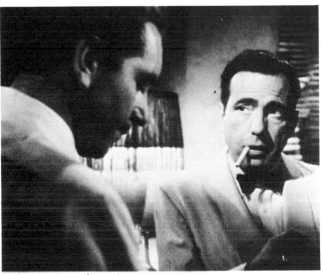

Rick: Yes. I get the point.

Laszlo: I wonder if you do. I wonder if you know that you're trying to escape from yourself and that you'll never succeed.

Rick: You seem to know all about my destiny.

Laszlo: I know a good deal more about you than you suspect.

211

Laszlo: I know, for instance, that you're in love with a woman. It is perhaps a strange circumstance that we should both love the same woman.

Laszlo: The first evening I came here to this cafe, I knew there was something between you and Ilsa.

Laszlo: Since no one is to blame, I, I demand no explanation.

Laszlo: I ask only one thing. You won't give me the Letters of Transit. All right. But I want my wife to be safe.

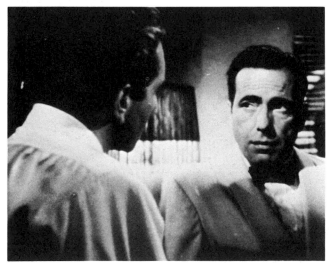

Laszlo: I ask you as a favor to use the letters to take her away from Casablanca.

Rick: You love her that much?

Laszlo: Apparently you think of me only as the leader of a Cause. Well, I'm also a human being. Yes, I love her that much.

Officer: Monsieur Laszlo?
Laszlo: Yes.
Officer: You'll come with us. We have a warrant for your arrest.

Laszlo: On what charge?
Officer: Captain Renault will discuss that with you later.

Rick: It seems that destiny has taken a hand.

Rick: You haven't any actual proof, and you know it. This isn't Germany or Occupied France. All you can do is fine him a few thousand francs and give him thirty days. You might as well let him go now.

Renault: Ricky, I'd advise you not to be too interested in what happens to Laszlo. If by any chance you were to help him to escape—
Rick: What makes you think I'd stick my neck out for Laszlo?

Renault: Because you've bet ten thousand francs he'd escape. Two, you've got the Letters of Transit.

Renault: Now don't bother to deny it. And, well, you might do it simply because you don't like Strasser's looks. As a matter of fact, I don't like him, either.

Rick: Well, they're all excellent reasons.

Renault: Don't count too much on my friendship, Ricky. In this matter I'm powerless.

Renault: Besides, I might lose the ten thousand francs.

Rick: You're not very subtle, but you are effective. I, I get the point. Yes, I have the letters, but I intend using them myself.

Rick: I'm leaving Casablanca on tonight's plane. The last plane.
Renault: What?

Rick: And I'm taking a friend with me. One you'll appreciate.
Renault: What friend?
Rick: Ilsa Lund.

Rick: That ought to put your mind to rest about my helping Laszlo escape. The last man I want to see in America.

Renault: You didn't come here to tell me this. You have the Letters of Transit. You can fill in your name and hers and leave anytime you please. Why are you still interested in what happens to Laszlo?

Rick: I'm not. But I am interested in what happens to Ilsa and me. We have a legal right to go, that's true, but people have been held in Casablanca in spite of their legal rights.
Renault: What makes you think we want to hold you?

Rick: Ilsa is Laszlo's wife. She probably knows things that Strasser would like to know. Louis, I'll make a deal with you.

Rick: Instead of this petty charge you have against him, you can get something really big, something that would chuck him in a concentration camp for years.

Rick: Be quite a feather in your cap, wouldn't it?

Renault: It certainly would. Germany, er, Vichy would be very grateful.
Rick: Then release him. You be at my place a half an hour before the plane leaves.

Rick: I'll arrange to have Laszlo come there to pick up the Letters of Transit and that'll give you the criminal grounds on which to make the arrest.

Rick: You get him, and we get away.

Rick: To the Germans that last will be just a minor annoyance.

Renault: There's still something about this business I don't quite understand. Miss Lund, she's very **beautiful**, yes, but you were never interested in any woman.

Rick: Well, she isn't just any woman.
Renault: I see. How do I know you'll keep your end of the bargain?

Rick: I'll make the arrangements right now with Laszlo, in the visitors' pen.

Renault: Ricky, I'm gonna miss you. Apparently you're the only one in Casablanca who has even less scruples than I.

Rick: Oh, thanks.
Renault: Go ahead, Rick.

Rick: And by the way, call off your watch-dogs when you let him go. I don't want them around this afternoon. I'm taking no chances, Louis, not even with you.

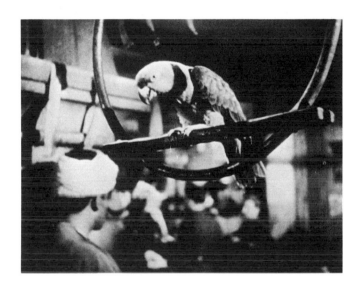

Ferrari: Shall we draw up papers or is our handshake good enough?

Rick: It's certainly not good enough, but since I'm in a hurry it'll have to do.

Ferrari: Oh, to get out of Casablanca and go to America! You're a lucky man.

Rick: Oh, by the way, my agreement with Sam has always been that he gets 25% of the profits. That still goes.

Ferrari: I happen to know he gets 10%. But he's worth 25.

Rick: And Abdul and Carl and Sacha, they stay with the place or I don't sell.

Ferrari: Of course they stay. Rick's wouldn't be Rick's without them.

Rick: Well, so long. Now don't forget, you owe Rick's a hundred cartons of American cigarettes.

Ferrari: I shall remember to pay it to myself.

Rick: You're late.

Renault: I was informed just as Laszlo was about to leave the hotel, so I knew I'd be on time.
Rick: I thought I asked you to tie up your watch-dogs.

Renault: Oh, he won't be followed here. You know, this place will never be the same without you, Ricky.
Rick: Yes, I know what you mean, but I've already spoken to Ferrari. You'll still win at roulette.

Renault: Is everything ready?
Rick: I've the Letters right here.

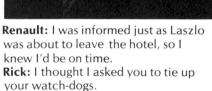

Renault: Tell me, when we searched the place, where were they?
Rick: In Sam's piano.

Renault: Serves me right for not being musical.

Rick: Oh, here they are. You better wait in my office.

Laszlo: Here.

Ilsa: Richard, Victor thinks I'm leaving with him. Haven't you told him?

Rick: No, not yet.
Ilsa: But it's all right, isn't it? You were able to arrange everything?

Rick: Everything is quite all right.
Ilsa: Oh, Rick—

Rick: We'll tell him at the airport. The less time to think the easier for all of us. Please trust me.

Ilsa: Yes, I will.

Laszlo: Monsieur Blaine, I don't know how to thank you.

Rick: Oh, save it. We've still lots of things to do.

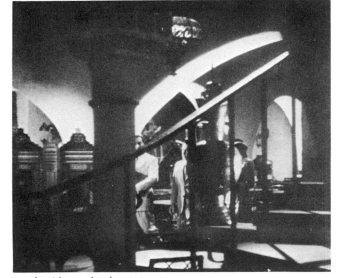

Laszlo: I brought the money.
Rick: Keep it. You'll need it in America.

Laszlo: But we made a deal.
Rick: Oh, never mind that. You won't have any trouble in Lisbon, will you?

Laszlo: No, that's all arranged.
Rick: Good. I've got the Letters right here. They're all made out in blank.

Rick: All you have to do is fill in the signatures.

Renault: Victor Laszlo! Victor Laszlo, you're under arrest.

Renault: On a charge of accessory to the murder of the couriers from whom these letters were stolen.

Renault: Oh, you're surprised about my friend Ricky? The explanation is quite simple.

Renault: Love, it seems, has triumphed over virtue.

Renault: Thank—

Rick: Not so fast, Louis. Nobody's going to be arrested. Not for a while yet.

Renault: Have you taken leave of your senses?

Rick: I have! Sit down over there!
Renault: Put that gun down!

Rick: Louis, I wouldn't like to shoot you, but I will if you take one more step.

Renault: Under the circumstances, I will sit down.

Rick: Keep your hands on the table.
Renault: I suppose you know what you're doing, but I wonder if you realize what this means?

Rick: I do. We've got plenty of time to discuss that later.
Renault: Call off your watch-dogs, you said!

Rick: Just the same, you call the airport and let me hear you tell them. And remember, this gun is pointed right at your heart!

Renault: That is my least vulnerable spot.

Renault: Hello? Is that the airport?

Renault: This is Captain Renault speaking. There'll be two Letters of Transit for the Lisbon plane.

Renault: There's to be no trouble about them. Good!

Strasser: Huh?

Strasser: Hello! Hello!

Strasser: My car, quickly!
Officer: Zu Befehl, Herr Major!

Strasser: This is Major Strasser. Have a squad of police meet me at the airport at once. At once! Do you hear?

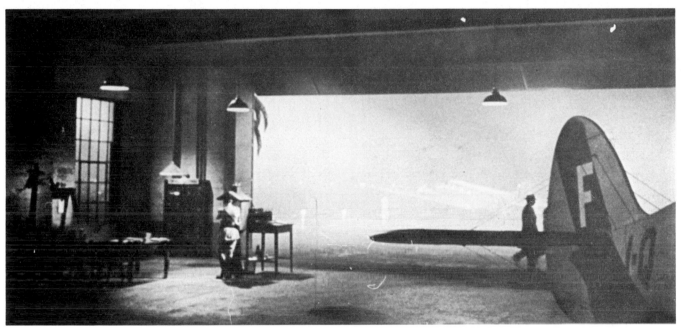

Orderly: Hello! Hello! Radio Tower! Lisbon plane taking off in ten minutes. East runway. Visibility one and one-half miles, light ground fog, depth of fog approximately five hundred, ceiling unlimited. Thank you.

Rick: Louis, have your man go with Mr. Laszlo and take care of his luggage.
Renault: Certainly, Rick. Anything you say.

Renault: Find Mr. Laszlo's luggage and put it on the plane.
Orderly: Yes, sir.

Orderly: This way, please.

Rick: If you don't mind, you fill in the names. That'll make it even more official.
Renault: You think of everything, don't you?

Rick: And the names are Mr. and Mrs. Victor Laszlo.

Ilsa: But, why my name, Richard?

Rick: Because you're getting on that plane.
Ilsa: I don't understand. What about you?

Rick: I'm staying here with him till the plane gets safely away.

Ilsa: No, Richard, no! What has happened to you? Last night we said —

Rick: Last night we said a great many things. You said I was to do the thinking for both of us. Well, I've done a lot of it since then and it all adds up to one thing. You're getting on that plane with Victor where you belong.

Ilsa: But Richard, no, I, I —

Rick: Now you've got to listen to me. Do you have any idea what you'd have to look forward to if you stayed here? Nine chances out of ten we'd both wind up in a concentration camp.

Rick: Isn't that true, Louis?

Renault: I'm afraid Major Strasser would insist.

Ilsa: You're saying this only to make me go.

Rick: I'm saying it because it's true. Inside of us we both know you belong with Victor. You're part of his work. The thing that keeps him going. If that plane leaves the ground and you're not with him, you'll regret it.

Ilsa: No.

Rick: Maybe not today, maybe not tomorrow, but soon, and for the rest of your life.

Ilsa: What about us?

Rick: We'll always have Paris. We didn't have it, we'd lost it until you came to Casablanca. We got it back last night.

Ilsa: And I said I would never leave you.

Rick: And you never will. But I've got a job to do, too. Where I'm going you can't follow. What I've got to do, you can't be any part of.

Rick: Ilsa, I'm no good at being noble, but it doesn't take much to see that the problems of three little people don't amount to a hill o' beans in this crazy world. Someday you'll understand that.

Rick: Now, now. Here's looking at you, kid.

Laszlo: Everything is in order.

Rick: All except one thing. There's something you should know before you leave.

Laszlo: Monsieur Blaine, I don't ask you to explain anything.

Rick: I'm going to, anyway, because it may make a difference to you later on.

Rick: You said you knew about Ilsa and me.
Laszlo: Yes.

Rick: But you didn't know she was at my place last night when you were. She came there for the Letters of Transit. Isn't it true, Ilsa?

Ilsa: Yes.

238

Rick: She tried everything to get them and nothing worked.

Rick: She did her best to convince me that she was still in love with me.

Rick: But that was all over long ago.

Rick: For your sake she pretended it wasn't, and I let her pretend.

Laszlo: I understand.

Rick: Here it is.

Laszlo: Thanks. I appreciate it.

Laszlo: Welcome back to the fight.

Laszlo: This time I know our side will win.

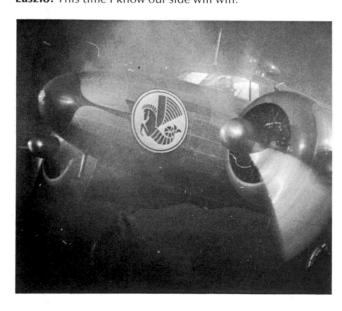

Laszlo: Are you ready, Ilsa?

Ilsa: Yes, I'm ready.

Ilsa: Goodbye, Rick.

Ilsa: God bless you.

Rick: You better hurry or you'll miss that plane.

Renault: Well, I was right. You are a sentimentalist!

Rick: Stay where you are! I don't know what you're talking about.

Renault: What you just did for Laszlo. And that fairy tale you invented to send Ilsa away with him. I know a little about women, my friend. She went, but she knew you were lying.

Rick: Anyway, thanks for helping me out.

Renault: I suppose you know this isn't going to be very pleasant for either of us, especially for you. I'll have to arrest you, of course.

Rick: As soon as the plane goes, Louis.

Strasser: What was the meaning of that phone call?

Renault: Victor Laszlo is on that plane.

Strasser: Why do you stand here? Why don't you stop him?

Renault: Ask Monsieur Rick.

Rick: Get away from that phone!

Strasser: I would advise you not to interfere.

Rick: I was willing to shoot Captain Renault and I'm willing to shoot you.

Strasser: Hello!

Rick: Put that phone down!

Strasser: Get me the Radio Tower.

Rick: Put it down!

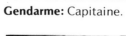
Gendarme: Capitaine.

Renault: Major Strasser's been shot. Round up the usual suspects.
Gendarme: Oui, mon Capitaine.

Gendarme: Prenez la voiture et allez avec lui.

 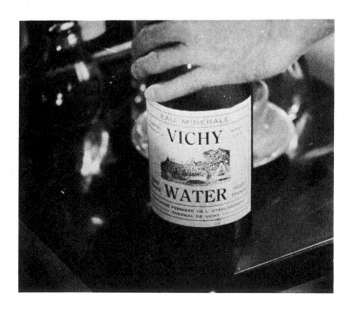

Renault: Well, Rick, you're not only a sentimentalist, but you've become a patriot.

Rick: Maybe, but it seemed like a good time to start.
Renault: I think perhaps you're right.

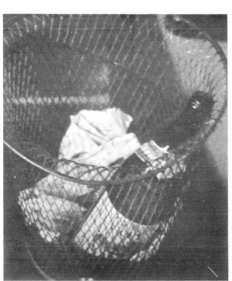

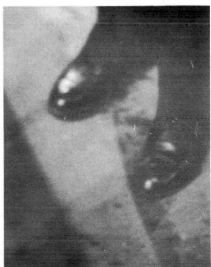

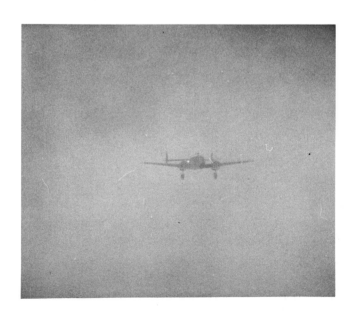 

Renault: It might be a good idea for you to disappear from Casablanca for a while.

Renault: There's a Free French garrison over at Brazzaville.

Renault: I could be induced to arrange your passage.

Rick: My Letter of Transit? I could use a trip, but it doesn't make any difference about our bet.

Rick: You still owe me ten thousand francs.

Renault: And that ten thousand francs should pay our expenses.

Rick: *Our* expenses?
Renault: Uh-huh.

Rick: Louis, I think this is the beginning of a beautiful friendship.